The Collected Poems
of Joyce Stein

JOYCE STEIN

THE COLLECTED POEMS

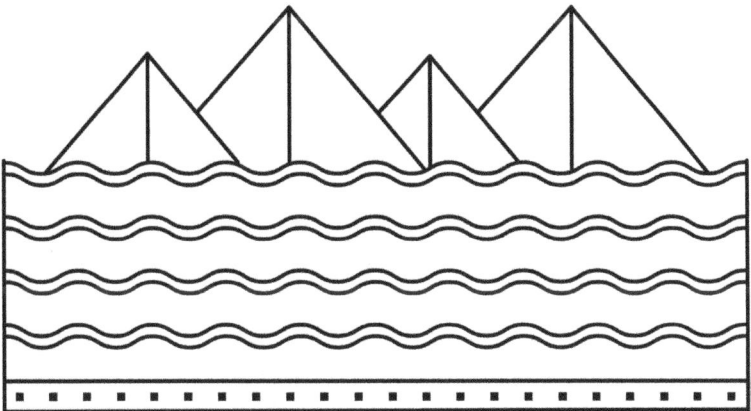

Copyright © 2021 Barney Stein
barn62@gmail.com

ISBN 978-0-578-96097-5

Edited and designed by Tell Tell Poetry

Printed in the United States of America

First Printing, 2021

Dedicated to my brothers, and to their wives and children, so they may have this record of our ancestor's life lived at the cusp of the millennium and her heart full of love for the humanity she found everywhere she went.

Contents

xi

Acknowledgments

The publication of this collection would not have been possible without the assistance of Kallie Falandays, who brought great skill and sensitivity to her reading, editing, and organization of the poems, and who gave me encouragement and space to make peace with the process I had before me. With gratitude,

—Barney Stein
April 30, 2021

The Collected Poems
of Joyce Stein

I
Skin of the Earth
Abroad

BEAUTIFUL

I don't know this young
person whose face
is not the perfection
of Greece,
the Western world,
but the buttery silkiness,
the eyes, the nose, bone
structure of Mongolia.

His arms are molded,
hairless, smooth legs
crossed at the knees
as he sits.
Turning to talk to his
sister, his friends, the
voice is higher
than I expected. Not
sweet but flat,
uninflected.

I can't
place him clearly
in the man/woman
spectrum.
Whoever he is,
he is beautiful.

BHUTAN HIGHWAY

Indian trucks outdo each other with garish colors painted
to the driver's taste, fringed with silver tinsel. With black
and white eyes outlined on fenders, a favorite deity cartooned
over the cab, they are Hindu exotics in Buddhist Bhutan.

Nepalese men break big rocks into pieces sized to fill potholes
that proliferate on the highway. Their wives wield hammers,
break stones by hand, while children climb dirt mounds.
The family home is a blue plastic tent on the road meridian.

A boy, branches strapped to his back, a walking tree, carries
feed for a cow or a horse his father rents to a trekker's guide.
Girls gather grasses, leaves, branches that edge the roadway,
dodge taxis and buses, transportation between the towns.

I see Indian men building houses, decorating facades with traditional
designs. Local women weave and sew in their second-floor quarters
above the cows and goats. Red chilis dry on tin roofs of these middle-
class homes and those of the huts that squat behind monasteries.

It's time for the Tsechu festival of Guru Rinpoche, the sainted Buddhist
teacher. Celebrants walk for miles, finely dressed women in draped *kiras*,
men in loosely wrapped ghos. Excited children push and chase each other.
Everyone has waited all year for this day—their only recreation.

We leave the road to follow them, crowd into the dzhong courtyard. Monks
twirl in ritual dances. Black hats, yellow hats, the costume tells a story,
invokes the deity to annihilate misfortune, grant wishes, purify the ground.
Drums boom, horns blare, monks chant, clowns cavort—a town party.

For three days they play; entertained, relaxed—then back to hard work.
I wonder if I could survive here. After the festival I'd have months
of no instant hot water, no dependable lights, or cars, or phones,
and no television—no CNN to clarify life in the third world.

ON THE BIG RED ISLAND

The tree limbs burn,
crackling as they go,
smoke and fumes
from the hot ash
swirling upward.

At the roadside, charcoal—gathered
like a crop from an old burn—
pokes through holes in worn sacks,
ready to heat the cooking pots
in crowded straw huts.

After the trees are gone,
the plot is leveled, flooded,
planted with a light green
nursery crop that darkens
as the rice matures.

Malagasy women will harvest the grain
to gain one more day, one more night,
perhaps to conceive another life.

When the rice no longer grows,
men fashion bricks
from the red clay,
bake them in the sun,
and sell them to buy
another, smaller plot of forest
until there is no more
on the big red island.

BLACKNESS

shines in the wet heat,
shimmers in contrast
to brilliant tribal robes
worn in the courts
of chiefs. Huge
umbrellas shade
the retinues of loyal
subjects on parade
before durbar pavilions,
escorted to designated spots.

Blackness is forest under tree canopies.
It is history: the beating,
the screaming of slaves
herded through castles
at the continental edge of Ghana.
Blackness is the bass sound
of drums beating the syllabic
rhythm of messages understood
by those who have learned to listen.
It is the birthright of Asante, Ga,
other tribes descended
from ancient kings,
lineages born in Africa,
honored in Africa.

BORNEO CAVE

Bats whistle, flutter below a chamber's vaulted ceiling.
I clutch wood, touch a slug-soft body, a centipede
with opaque eyes, puckered flesh pale in a circle of light.
Near my hand tiny bats sway, heads down, wrinkled wings
creased above pinched snouts, open jaws, pointed teeth.

Electric bulbs mark hard-packed dirt trails, weave around
stalagmites, color-lit, bearing tourist titles: *Zeus' throne*
or *seraglio curtain*. We go deeper, into shadowy echoing
chambers to see what cavemen saw, feel what they felt.

> Douse all lights.
> Experience ancient black
> deep as breath,
> chilled as death.
> Light-quick to shatter the dark,
> run toward the sun.

Desiccated bones, skeletons; brushed, labeled, museum-
bound, and we know only rock wall sketches, faded
charcoal or iron red outlines of horses and elk, crude creations
by artists at a fraction's distance from the entrance arch.

Uneven stones outline burial sites where I stand,
a shadow's edge from the cave mouth. Young and old
once ventured out, drawn by warm sunlight, greenery
with hidden fruit, branches that fell, dried into tinder
for glowing fires that warmed a narrow, starlit world.

BUILDERS OF THE TEMPLE

Laborers tore their hands,
bound the mortar with
their blood, added a red
outline to the rose brick,
the carvings of the spirits,
wall decorations of this tenth
century women's temple.

Workmen's sons soldiered;
workmen's daughters served,
their duty to the king,
the glory of the dynasty,
the honor of the Khmer people.

After the battles, after
this king was deposed,
the gods remembered
who built this temple
and granted their prayers.

The trees of the Cambodian
jungle have broken the walls;
the carvings, delicate
but worn, are a hint to us
of the beauty that was here.

Gods are remembered so long
as people believe; the builders,
the workmen, their sons
and daughters,
all are long-forgotten.

A TRAVELLER'S VIEW

The Taj Hotel lobby, caramel-colored
leather sofas, gilded tables, carpets
woven in a Kolkata factory by children
nimble in near-darkness.
Bar patrons, sheltered in filtered air,
chat over the clink of ice cubes,
dine later, first visit a museum
with ancient carvings, Moghul paintings.

Turbaned Sikhs, doormen eye hotel guests
as they trickle out onto a Mumbai sidewalk.
A beggar wears a ruin of harlequin, pantaloons
embedded with mica in dirt, grovels, holds
a grimy palm up for a tourist's rupee.
His leprous companion waves a stump
of arm, thrusts the rounded end of a bone
upwards toward lowered eyes.

Tourists draw together, warned:
*the sidewalk world is one
of fraud and trickery.*

BABI YAR

Finnair had lost permission to land in Kiev, so I flew to Riga to
    catch a Latvian
shuttle and missed the first half day, so assistant tour guide, Barbara,
took me to visit Babi Yar.

Barbara, thinking her Ukrainian name too difficult for American
    tongues, asked why
people thought it important—more than important, necessary—to
    visit Babi Yar.
"There's nothing there but a big statue and an empty field."

She was young, even so, how could she have been born here, lived
    here, and not understood about Babi Yar . . .

I explained as we walked around the statue. It was massive, grotesque,
    made of metal shapes resembling body parts, all stuck together.
    Plaques in three languages—Hebrew, Russian, and English—
    told the story of the thousands slaughtered here: Jews, gypsies,
    communists, dissenters, all were murdered on this spot. Their
    nameless corpses were covered with earth. All of the officials, all
    of them, had tried to conceal what had happened here.

"My father was born in Kiev," I said, "Possibly a relative of mine is
    buried here.
I believe the spirits of these murdered people still weep here."

Barbara confessed that nothing about this was taught as part of
    Ukrainian history. I was certain it was not. Discussion means
    facing truths. Facing truths means admitting
culpability, which leads to guilty feelings and other unpleasantness.

"I want to show you something," Barbara said and led me down a
    path paved with
round stones, maybe fifty meters or so, to a pedestal on which
    stood a tall menorah,
each arm ending in an electric light bulb.

"It's lit sometimes," she said. "I don't know when or why. They choose the times. The city put it here as a memorial. I understand now, better. I never read the plaques before.

I didn't know so many people cared."

CLIMBING CHOMOLUNGMA

From base camp, the top of Everest
didn't look that daunting
but custom and belief came in
—one woman dreamt
of monks, an augury of danger,
death. She stayed behind.

Facing the mountain, its whiteness
broken by black stone ridges,
two women, with male helpers,
climbed higher, over ladders
laid for traction across ice bridges.
Unsure of what awaited—it could be fog
or heavy winds—they pursued their dream.
Pinnacles are Loreleis,
they lure despite the danger.

One made it to the top, brandished
her triangular red felt banner,
triumphant, planted it on the peak.
She earned the fame she needed
to prove her worth, improve her
status in the tribe—the first Sherpa
woman to summit and descend—alive.

Her companion descended too soon.
Towards the top, the wind tore her breath
from her lungs—even with the oxygen,
her toes and fingers stung,
her legs began to shake,
her head to ache; hallucinations
hovered on the edge of vision.

CROSSING BORDERS

The palm leaf thatch casts delicious
shade, cools my sweaty face, hot
from the trek along the crumbling irrigation
ditches, behind the "short-cut" lady who knew
the best way through fields cleared of sugar cane.

With a gesture, the boss invites us to sit around
the table, welcomes us in his spare English—
we wouldn't understand his native Pa'O.
He offers us green tea from a thermos
and slices of the molasses candy he makes here.
Our trousers confuse them—are we women?
Longyis, Myanmar dress, they understand.

Some of the family rests with us. Two boys
appear, shed their backpacks, tear off their shirts,
climb the piles of cane stalks. Then they head
for the running creek to cool off
before joining the men to stoke the fires
with dried stalks and keep the pots boiling.

Our guide, Nang Mar Lar, tells us about
her grandmother's best friend who lives
in this village. They have not seen each other
for years. The villages are a six-hour walk
apart, and the bullock carts are reserved
for bringing cane to the mill and baskets
filled with molasses candy to the market.

She is to bring news of the woman's
well-being. The family tells us where
to find her on the way back to our boat.
It is time to leave. We take photos.
The women primp. The kids grin.
The men try not to look too eager.

Each day here attaches to the next
like the cars of a train moved by the rhythm
of the work that fills the daylight hours
until the season ends, the cane runs out,
and planting begins for another crop.

This is the work they are born into.
It is their past and their future.
We are only a small diversion
as we pass through their present.

DRAGON WALL

Blackened by age, his body
crowns the length of the wall
that encloses this garden
created by a poet centuries ago
as a place for contemplation
of philosophy and life.

The dragon is as I remember him:
nostrils flaring, gentle in his fierceness,
protecting a small creature
between his paws.

Outside his world of rocks
and flowers, pavilions, carvings,
bridges, fish, and twisted trees,
the old Shanghai has disappeared.

The sprawling mall
backs up to his garden.
Silk scarves, ties, slippers, and shirts;
vendors of teas, Mandarin coats,
chopsticks, rice bowls, woven hats, and fans
fill the stalls along serpentine alleys.

The tourists and natives
are boisterous as they shop,
bargaining for each purchase
as though their lives depended on it.
Some follow the curve
of the wall into the garden.

It wasn't what the poet wanted:
tired shoppers comparing buys,
eager children climbing rocks,
throwing bread onto water.

I think the dragon knows
he's lucky
to have survived this long,
this tiny bit of beauty his to guard.

ENTERTAINMENT

Crickets buzz a vibrant alarm;
she wakes, rolls off her mat
to start the fire, fetch river
water in her oilcan, cook
the few withered stalks
while village children watch,
their pinched owl-like faces
tight under reddened curls.

Chores fill the day, but tonight
the headman will power
up their television, show
flickering pictures like last week's—

white girls in tight blue suits
jumped, arms rising to the beat
of western music; a grinning
woman wove past soft chairs,
fed grains to plump children;
a red auto streaked around
curves, the driver's gesture
at the car, the woman beside
him, meant all was his.

Tonight she will sigh, black skin
glistening in pale artificial light,
dream with all the villagers
of finding such a place
where someone else lights
the fire, sweeps the hard-
packed dirt floor, provides
succulent food—but beyond
that, she longs for the cars,
clothes, soft furniture, all
marvelous possessions
found in the western world.

EVERYTHING CHANGES/
NOTHING CHANGES

Three ancient sports claim honor in this Naadam festival,
fill three days with male competition. Boy jockeys race
horses for miles, dooming some horses. Wrestlers pound
muscled arms against bare chests. Archers aim, strain
against the bow's weight, rip arrows into red targets.

In Ulaanbaatar, determined drivers lust for challenge,
bore into traffic, force new positions, twist onto sidewalks,
secure a brief advantage by the width of a fender's paint.
Swarms attack the outer roads, like the hordes Chinggis,
great khan, sent 800 years ago to father Mongolia.

We shunt off from the aggressive autos, head for a camp-
ground where tents and gers on a green meadow await us.
I mount a small Mongolian horse, a prop for photos.
Royal in borrowed brocade and crown, I smile through
dangling strings of beads. The men, leather clad,
glower with fierce faces under spiked helmets.

Now comes the promised horhog, feast
for warriors and queens, an entire sheep cut open
gullet to tail, filled with burning rocks, roasted
from the inside out, entrails, liver, kidneys. Bones
rise up from steaming flesh, muscles tied by gristle.

Everyone nibbles organ meat, chews stringy, sweeter
flesh, swallows soup from the bottom of the pot.
Our feeble plastic forks are no match for tough flesh.
Hands tear the meat, devour it while gurgling
down beer after beer. Youngsters pass vodka,
the only Russian legacy Mongolians enjoy.

As clouds grey the sky, purple spills from the hills,
creeps into shadows on the grass. Bleary with

mutton and beer, spinning with outstretched arms,
we acknowledge the spirits of ancient Asia.

Everything changes. Nothing changes.
We gird our psyches for tumultuous traffic,
a return to our temporary homes, call out
"Thank you and goodbye—
bayarlalaa, bayartai."

HUNZA VALLEY

Steep hillsides are terraced with a patchwork
        of tiny family plots outlined by rubble walls.
Each farm is green with vines that carry heavy orange
        squashes or their long and floppy flowers.
Harvested potatoes, wrenched from the earth, are shoved
        into burlap sacks by grunting sons
and neighbors, tossed into the bed of a beat-up truck
        that sprang from a generation
of mismatched parts and frayed wires. Top heavy,
        the rusty jalopy moves slowly, a senior.
The jeeps are the kids in the 'hood, with drivers
        who challenge the rutted dirt roads.

High tors border the sky with their grey shards.
        They name their price for being conquered.
From the pinnacle of Ladyfinger, a Japanese
        climber fell to his death yesterday.
Across the Hunza Valley rises Rakaposhi peak.
        Ultar I and Ultar II bare their faces
to the thin sun. Their makeup is snow that melts
        daily, refreezes at night. All the peaks
nest stars between their ridges, until at 5 a.m.
        the shell of night cracks open,
and the yolk of the sun spurts into day again,
        bringing light, colorless and clean.

Inside the huts, everyone wakes. Children leave
        to watch the cattle graze, flicking them
with thin branches. Adults, kneeling, perform
        the first of five daily prayers.
Once separate kingdoms shared the valley.
        Now the Shiites, Sunnis, and a few Ismailis
segregate themselves into enclaves, huddle
        for protection from each other.

Buddha stopped at the border when the Chinese
        road builders who spread his ethic went away.
Ancient Hindu gods are disavowed. India and Pakistan
        skirmish with each other across the Punjab.

The natives who have never left this valley all believe
        those who stay here any length of time
and try to climb the mountains—like the foreigners
        who fled from Shangri-La—
that they who are real but restless in Eden
        will forfeit Paradise forever.

IMAGINE

This day is a song transposed into a minor
key. Wind-driven rain rips ragged the edges
of sycamore leaves, swells them to yellow
into the brown of winter when few
will be left clinging. Lichen patches glow
greenish-white, ghost-light decorations,
covering dents where fallen twigs left scars.

Once white, the wall is streaked with dirty
rivulets, pulled by gravity
into brown pools below the gate. Wearing
a hooded coat, clutching my umbrella,
I could pass through that gate, curious.

Imagine what lies beyond the wall:
grass, leftover from spring, red and purple
blooms clinging to flower stalks, houses
with neat lawns, secure behind square hedges.

Imagine wandering much farther,
overseas, by dirt yards, mud huts;
strangers who smile, accept my handshake.
Survival consumes their days, but they
still find time for singing together.

Imagine the road ending. I face
about, return to the wall from
the other side. Curious. Wondering
what lies beyond the wall.

LEMURS

The round eyes of sifakas
stare at me out of small faces,
the smooth black skin a contrast
to the cream-colored bunting
of fur that ends above black paws.
Arms waving for balance, they dance
on crooked toes, between the trees,
through patches of sunlight and shade.
Their rear legs are too long
to let them travel on all fours.

In an isolated grove,
the indri bellow, an ear-splitting
call to warn another family
of our intrusion. Our tourist
bananas will only work on them.

At night, mouse lemurs curl up,
hiding in the elbows of the trees.
Their eyes glow red, reflect the beams
from flashlights human stalkers use.

I see crowned lemurs poke black
widow's peaks through chain-link
fences so scientists can watch
and study them. Madagascar
is the only home the lemurs have.
Mauritius, island of extinction,
where the dodo disappeared,
is not that far away.

OZYMANDIAS, AGAIN

from Shelley

Desert sands slip
in the wind,
mound next to
settlement walls,
blasted-out homes,
the razor wire of camps.
Along these borders,
a black carpet,
cluster of flies,
creeps slowly
over the humps
of severed limbs.
Tribes, in the name
of a god,
a book,
a history,
demand the sole right
to exist here.
Corrupted,
the desert blooms
into bombs, rockets
that twist steel,
leave trunkless legs.

Ozymandias long ago
boasted of his kingdom,
taunted mighty kings.
He, too, paid
for his arrogance,
left trunkless legs,
but his were
made of stone.

PARIS NO. 1

A wild ride at 3 a.m. from Le Bourget, a modicum of French, and
    extra tips
had made the lady taxi driver come alive, dash madly: time is francs.

Wheels swerved, I bounced between two large male bodies, one a
    husband,
one a traveling friend, protection from the worn upholstery on the
    steel sides.

Yellow lights haloed by mist that swirled around fogged-up glass
    enclosures,
amber jewels set on ornate metal posts; heads and arms of stone
    statues lining
bridges over the Seine, all of this was here and so was I, glimpsing
    upper parts
of everything through the windows streaked with city grime.

Early morning was the only quiet time we found. We spent days
    seeking out
the famous and spectacular: *Winged Victory*, the *Venus*, *Mona Lisa* at
    the Louvre.
From Notre Dame we went to Sainte Chapelle, a wonder in itself, a
    huge kaleidoscope,
the reds, the blues, the purples, everywhere in varied combination.
    And I drowned in it.

We visited an old church, Saint-Germain-des-Prés. An organist was
    playing, just
rehearsing for a concert, and we stayed to listen, staring at the
    ceiling of a
darkened powder-blue, gold stars scattered through the gilded,
    wooden strips.

Eiffel Tower. Champs Elysees, where I found a chestnut fallen from above
and carried it away, a souvenir. The paths along the river where booksellers
had their stalls. Les Halles (or what was left of it) to buy the copper pots.

Days stuffed with new experiences, almost filled the pockets of
  omnipresent doubts.
Nights we nearly shared the mutual qualms we'd carried with us in
  forgetfulness.

Time whirled away and left at last the day to leave, go home, see
  our children.
Souvenirs would be memories, photographs, a daily journal. The
  chestnut I had kept
was broken, its shell cracked and unprotective—I threw it out. The
  hotel room was
ordinary. Outside the window was still Paris, but it could have been
  almost any place.

FISHERMAN

The Greek whiteness of the stucco wall
(gray in early morning light)
defined, with the window, a shadow box,
framing a sea view to the horizon.
At the center, midway to the skyline,
a rowboat floated, a local,
fishing just before dawn.

The boat was too far away
to hear the slap of the waves
and the ping of the spray
against the hull. A lantern
bobbed up and down, shone
at the prow, losing its brightness
as daylight blanched the sky.
The fisherman came ashore
prepared to bargain for his price,
a harder job than fishing.

THE VISIT

The pure African faces are so black
they are almost blue, with contours
that blend into the hut's interior.
Black etched onto still more black.
Breath defines the space where
faces are; unseen, easy to imagine.
I picture them masked, with broad
noses, full lips smooth, but not the skin.
Not satisfied with the gentle curves
of cheeks and forehead, they drew
lines upon them, cut into the flesh,
let the blood drip over their chins.
They filled the slits with dirt, the
painful scars swelled into a design,
the chosen beauty marks of tribal
pride, identity, village tradition.

Light leaks in beneath the thatch,
between the woven rushes of the
door. My eyes absorb the light and
cast it back. I see their eyes gleam,
but there is no flash of teeth,
no glint from open mouths,
no cheering grin of greeting,
nothing I can see that tells
me I am welcome here. Flash
bulbs shoot around me making
fuzzy lightning, deepening
the contrast with the
blackness that absorbs the light.

They believe my lens can capture
bodies, make them prisoners inside
my little box. They fear the shrinking
of their selves, the diminution of
their souls, the capture of their

spirits, leaving them no longer
free to fly around the room
like Tinker Bells in silhouette.

I might steal their hidden selves and
carry them to some place far away
and hostile, leaving only husks
without an inner life, unable to
enjoy the contact with their gods.

Our good guide told them in his
Wolof tongue, or French patois,
that we should be allowed to
visit. We are friends, we come
to study Africa, the village life,
to learn their customs and their
secrets, things their elders
tell them only they should
know about or understand.

No matter, we will not learn
much or hear the deepest of
their thoughts. We enter,
snap our photographs of
huts, but this is not their
private world. We cannot
touch their minds. Their
deepest thoughts will not
be shared, not even with
each other, least of all with us.

They stretch their hands
out, palms upturned, much
paler than their arms. We
give a coin or two and what
a bargain. Cheap at any price,
but here, for us, it's just the
going rate for souls.

PHOTOGRAPHS

Photographs, replaced sequentially
in their envelopes, are album bound.
Someone might ask to see them.

A grinning woman squinting into sunlight,
waving at the faraway camera's undiscerning lens.
A man, face shadowed by a gondolier's hat,
posed on a bridge over a troubled canal.
Scenes of a river that, roiling around boulders,
tossed flotsam, the photographer tried to censor.
Clouds, sheltering an over-bright disc of a sun,
so far set, its rays barely color the grey, cottony bottoms.

Rapidly developed. A special order.
It's just as well. Her emotions weaken to arm's
length with each photo scanned. It's a struggle
to recapture the feeling of exhilaration.

The treachery of memory is here.
When did she wear that blouse (too Fuji-blue
for her earth-tone-loving skin)?
All those wrinkles, so prominent across her cheeks
as she stands before a monastery's ancient ruins.
That tall woman, what was her name, the one who was cheerful,
friendly, wanted her address, but forgot to ask?

Her smile hides with the pictures,
the glow on her face coalesces into the glowering day.

PICK ANOTHER FLOWER

Drought browns the cracked land
leaving an oasis—Kirstenbosch,
where South Africa's pride, the king
protea explodes into peach and gold,
tended, cherished in this garden.

Manicured paths wind away from
the border of upper-class homes,
down into the dirt alleys,
the township of "informal" housing,
haphazard scatter of shanties.

Woman. She twists her way
between lean-tos of wood, scrap
tin, cardboard, enters an uncurtained
door into her home of peeling
walls papered with tin can labels.

Child, balanced on the woman's hips,
clings to the shawl carrier, head banging
against her mother. She whimpers
as the mother, quick with purpose,
carries what she can, runs away.

Fears of the plague in her body,
the future of her unborn child,
of more beatings, force her to choose:
hard city streets or inhospitable bush.

PICTURE SCULPTURE

crafted with care,
rose above the plane
as Japanese lace-like shapes,
a thinly layered bridge,
footpath; humans,
flattened yet delicate,
all made of rice:
cooked, sticky, sculpted.

A lengthy project,
hours spent culminating
in this solitary viewing,
the cost of creation.
I felt fulfilled if only for
a single moment.

It was worth it,
a measure of its value
my deep satisfaction.

A rare moment,
in a time of effort and disappointment,
of expectations unrealized,
savored again, remembered.

Moment over, a sudden
waking from my reverie,
I slaked my unforeseen,
intense hunger,
devoured the entire
rice sculpture.

PIERROT

White-faced clown
with triangular
eyebrows peaking
into a high forehead,

fingertips that
pick an arachnid
dance, a piccato
tarantella,

satin pantaloons,
blouse over loose knees,
paddling feet,
handled
by un-French masters.

Powder-puff
buttons jiggle
when a buckling
chest collapses
over a heap of limp strings.

To play out the comedy,
Pierrot must arise,
pirouette,
entertain,
conclude
with a puppet embrace.

ROMANIA

Part 1
Hilde

The dark mahogany table, matching
credenza, highlight the light-colored
photos: a man in military, then civilian
dress; the frames multiple, prominent.
Hilde's late husband, love of her life,
always admired, never forgotten.
Tonight, Hilde wears flamboyant faux
leopard dress, leopard shoes, purse,

earrings; dressed for him, lush, feminine.
We party at a farewell to Sibiu,
not all Romania. Speeches, toasts,
gourmet eating, picture taking,
old-school hand kissing, delightful.
Hilde dashes, greets, introduces
spouses. I chatter to everyone, share
highlights of my Sibiu visit with new

friends. Over the past days,
we shared personal life events:
siblings, parental horror stories,
fears for our children, clarified history,
confusion about our futures.
People separated by culture,
language—all colored
by the brush of humanity.

Too soon good-byes, regrets, promises
to e-mail and we return to Hilde's
in a sudden downpour echoing
sadness of separation. In Sibiu
I shared something of myself,
released the safety valve of silence,

sometimes easier with strangers
than with old companions.

Part 2
Painted Monasteries

Fifteenth century monasteries, walls
choked with bible stories, creation
of strange creatures, more heart than
artistry. A red swath swooshes down
to a wider bottom, devil portrayed
in flames with scary features,
threat to unbelievers; peasants,
illiterate, learning their bible
from the priests and these drawings,
felt fear of disobeying the church.

Martyrs, all sainted now, pictured
in gory detail, flayed alive,
headless, blood dripping, display
that all shown here is what they
died for. Paintings, supposed
to feature blue paint made of
pulverized lapis lazuli stones
was never brilliant, now is faded.
This building, dedicated to a religious
hermit, Daniel, is entered through
a door near his image.

Glittering with gold, walls, arches
domed ceilings repeat biblical
stories from the exterior including
Old Testament tales, Moses out
of Egypt. Archangels, draped
over doorways, military saints.
Three rooms, walls entirely covered,
velvet draperies reveal predictable
mother and child. Nuns in white-

rimmed wimples watch us. There
has been graffiti on these walls.
One nun, young with lovely skin,
has penciled eyebrows, a touch
of mascara. She points out,
explains certain figures, icons.

Interruptions. Tour groups, most
of the regular visitors here,
interrupt each other with loud
explanations of the interior pictures
for the ears of their group. Languages
loudly mix, make it hard to distinguish
words. Rudeness is rife; we leave
to continue outside. These quiet,
preserved monasteries have
all the company they need.

Part 3
Danube Delta

Flowing by Bucharest, past small cities,
villages, the Danube delivers its load
of crushed plastic bottles, billowing
bags, rotted vegetation into the Black Sea.
The delta, wide with narrow waterways,
intricate channels fit out slow shallow
boats, passing Ukrainian cattle-raising
farms. Farm houses, dull common wood,
brick, are unlike the bright stuccoed
suburban homes we saw farther north,
proliferating in fuchsia, orange, yellow,
chartreuse, moss green. Smells from
farms accompany the plopping of cow
excrement into water. Trucks, autos
delineate roads traversing the delta
parallel to the river. Lunch at a fisherman's
house is seriously boiled local fish in broth.

Quiet channel, no buildings, heaven for bird
lovers. Lolling back in the boat, we pull over
to flowering lily pads with little green frogs.
Thick reeds, a refuge for papery white egrets
stalking tiny fish, line the mud banks. Speckled
snake wiggles across the surface seeking muskrat
or small birds. Cormorants' black necks stick
straight up, dive on sight. Willows bordering
banks hide a small heron, a brown bittern.
Before main channel, a white swan with
three cygnets is joined by the cob, paddling fast,
heading, like us, back to reality, to spot-docked

Romanian naval vessels used here to seek
poachers of river-bound sturgeon for their caviar
or hailing ocean-bound, Romanian-built Dutch
ships bound for Somalia, pirate-hunting.
Port guardians, as in Roman days when warehouses
piled up saleable goods; they have had, since 1984,
no communist threat to shipping. Unknown
futures require the gray presence of
small, but armed, deterrents.

Peace on the river versus war awareness.

RYOKAN POOL

We women bathe in tepid,
transparent water.
Nakedness muddles
the place in society
clothing assigns to us.

No language means
no way to share tales
of grandchildren, magotachi,
boast of their achievements,
complain about husbands.

I squeeze my palms together,
squirt water into startled faces.
They grin, squirt back.
Taking turns, we spray each
other, try for greater distance.

Giggles need no tongue.
Nods, smiles help us share
our quiet time soaking.
Naked, saying sayonara
I glide into my private cubicle.

SALT CATHEDRAL

Through Stygian darkness, the tunnel slants down and down.
In slow descent we marvel at the work of Colombian miners,
their use of bodies and machines to blast and dig, deliver
salt by cart and elevator to a needy world. Salt, nature's
creation, preserver of freshness, feeder of men.

The miners, locals from Zipaquirá, breathed air pumped
in, as it is today. When the salt petered out, they created
an offering, carved out stations of the cross, eerily glowing
in greenish light, identified by Roman numerals, set off
from the tunnel by low walls, kneeling pads. Hard rock

for worshippers. Each cross bears a singular mark,
a trimmed end here, a slash there, designed
with care to suggest the procession along
the Via Dolorosa—Jesus fell, staggered here,
bore the scourge, fell again, stumbled on.

The tunnel opens into huge caverns. Pews,
benches, empty stages await congregations.
Free-standing statues of Mary, Joseph, Satan,
animals. Angels are raised up, stare down.

Miners burned out their bodies, gave their blood
to construct this world wonder. Colombians are
proud to honor the minds that envisioned it.
The women of Zipaquirá sell souvenirs
fashioned of salt—nature's creation,
preserver of freshness, feeder of men.

SEGESTA

Pediments are streaked
with rust-colored stains
from centuries of storms, tops
so crusted with crumbled stones
that crows must pick a pathway
through, but if the perch becomes
treacherous, they fly before they fall.

The earliest Greek settlers raised
this temple, left deep cylinders,
pillar-shaped in the quarried earth,
built an altar for sacrifices
to pay homage to a god, slake
his bone hunger, insure his favor.
This edifice, towering, fearsome
in its height, position, was meant
to terrorize Athenian
troops if they came from the sea.

They sailed toward Sicily,
grim battlers, weary, middle-aged
even in their youth, returning
to die in middle age until
Athens understood:

> Conquest must be swift
> or we must be content
> to live long years
> among a hostile people.

SHOPPING TRIP

Vendors surround us, jostle each
other, thrust their wares closer.
I look past the crude carvings,
the flimsy baskets balanced
on the pale palms of their hands,
hands that are calloused, not from
weaving grass or whittling animal images,
but from gleaning the stubble of meager harvests.

I don't look down, either.
To look down is to acknowledge
broken shoes, protruding toes,
dirty heels, or ankles red with sores.
T-shirts from Ohio State and knitted
caps from Michigan replace their tribal skirts.

I have mastered marketplace demeanor:
I look just above their ears,
as though seeking someone far away.
I walk with an *I-know-where-I'm-going* pace.
I glance sidelong at the merchandise
and ask for prices only if I really want to buy.
I bargain for each cent.
All natives want to cheat us, I was told,
even though they call me "mother"
out of respect, the guide says.

Back at the bus,
we compare our prizes and the prices paid.
Some of us gloat over bested artisans
and glower at anyone who paid a lower price.

We slouch deep into our seats.
Bargaining is hard work
and lunch waits for us
at our hotel.

SKIN OF THE EARTH

Tall trees long ago went for burning
in this rural Ireland of cold, dry nights;
no sound, not even crickets. Curly-leaved
ground cover stretches away from this dirt path.

Bogs here, bogs, where tales told by archeologists
and diggers turn into storylines—one female body,
interred, skin leathered, gaping mouth toothless,
yearning toward her final breath of air, intrigues
researchers into human information. No need
for answers, the find is the glory they can print.

Trench diggers, workers with traditional spades,
now mount wide-tired machines, straddle ditches
to dig peat, pile it into heaps of bricks. People here,
soldiers of life, burn them for heat, cooking,

uses from another time. I discover the link,
Olde to newe, of survival in a limited landscape.
Smoke rises. The dark is from bog fuel,
the temporary white from twigs, branches.

The skin of the earth. Dig into it, it will not bleed or flinch
from the point of a pickaxe, slicing blade, shovel's square cut.
Earth's bowels have been blasted, blown out.
The covering skin provides, every year, a little less.

SONG OF THE CARGO CULT

Wait for the engines to stop turning,
the gangplank to hit the dock
before you try to board the vessel.
Wait for the bounty,
the sacks of flour and sugar,
the burlap bags bulging with spuds,
the boxes of cans, crates
of apples for the mess halls,
and, even better, the cartons of
cigarettes: Luckies, Camels,
all the old familiar brands.

Work for the army, the navy,
anyone who needs strong backs
and arms. The pay's okay,
but it's the supplies
that are the real gold,
stashes to sell on the streets
of Port Moresby or Madang.

Who needs to labor in the fields,
toil with the muck in pigsties,
sweat out the rains,
when all you have to do
is show up at the right time
and gather the reward?
After they unload the ammo
and the small brass pick the plums,
there's plenty left for everyone else
as long as they're close by.

So it was, and so it will be again,
all you need to do is wait,
and someday the planes will land,
the ships will dock.

And the dreams
of wives and kids,
houses and farms,
tribal pride?

Stacked in the corners
of deserted warehouses
where Norwegian rats
and mold can eat them away.

Keep the lanterns at hand.
Kerosene may have to do
to light up the pot-holed
runways, the rotting docks,
the rutted dirt roads.

The white guys, providers
of supplies, will come again,
and when they do, we must be ready
to welcome them.

SPIRIT SHIELD

Hanging down my wall,
the carved shield ellipses
around a moon-like
face. Unlidded eyes
peer over pierced nostrils
down to a bat's head.

The young Papuan
understood payback,
knew spirit calling
to be far
beyond his reach.
Unless—
he held the shield out,
it belong me haus. Me laikim sell
halpim me pliz.

Shield money bought him
vengeance in his world.

In our world—we
deal the death card.
The black queen
confirms—revenge
shall happen.
Shells explode.
Villages burn.
We are ordained to do
our own
killing.

TATTOOS

decreed by ancient
councils still stain the old
woman's chin, feather
her forehead, bruise
with purple her face
as she bends to earth
facing Mecca.
Five times a day, she
is the only one at prayer
in this household of women.

A small granddaughter
with frizzy hair pulled
into two puffs learns French,
English, Arabic in her Koran
studies, plays with friends,
dances free in denim pants
or short, ruffled dress.

In a few years she will
twist her hair into a bun,
bind it with a scarf
so no tendril escapes, hide
her young body under a loose,
flowing jilbab so she can
walk outdoors with women.

Temporary tattoos, hennaed
hands will still celebrate
her family, her tribe.

THE CHOSEN

An old man, born
to farm, lifts his fists,
threatens heaven's gates,
demands his Lord stop
the floods that wash away
his crops. After two years
of drought, now the land
is a quagmire. Fenceposts
rot beneath the ground
until the fence collapses,
leaving him unprotected.

His face a mask of terrible
anger, he makes a last appeal.
He cries for justice, equity,
commiseration—his due
for the worship of a lifetime.

The god he created has no
ear for his pleading.
He is not a zealot.
He is not a madman,
not one of those
who kills for the right
to be the chosen of his god.

ASHKELON

Hava and Ari, my hosts, remind
me—tonight there is shul, do I attend?
High holy days only, but I want
the Israeli experience. Hava demurs,
doesn't approve of separation
of women, so I go with Ari,
who joins the men all reading at once,
bowing over their Hebrew texts.

Ushered into a small back room
with a loudspeaker connection,
I meet a single young woman
there who is surprised to have
a companion. I tell her I am
not orthodox, do not know
Hebrew. "Do what I do,
follow me," she says

This becomes a long, loud
physical sharing experience,
which is, after all, one of the
reasons I am in Ashkelon.

Much later Ari and I walk home.
I ask, "You live so near Gaza,
do you ever cross the border?"

"On behalf of an Israeli client,
only if it is absolutely
necessary. It is complicated,
with Hamas involved and
I don't know any Palestinians."
I do not ask why.

ASHKELON MEMORIAL

The night curtain will not part to reveal
the future, but behind the readers lights
will blossom, one by one, beneath memorial
photos, as they iterate the names
to resurrect the past.

There is Mordecai, dead on a numbered hill;
Eliahu, shot, left bleeding in the dirt;
Haya, daughter of Esther, captured,
then she disappeared.
The two sons of Ezra, called Ben Ezra,
known as Marcus and as Ephraim,
burned in an exploding bunker.
Zvi, who bent to help a wounded
friend, never stood erect again.
Ruth and Orit
Shlomo and Noah.
Their names are called in a span of
minutes, short like their span of years.

They once stood with pride,
ready to exchange their mortarboards for red
berets, become expensive pawns
who knew the moves but not the plan.
Left off strategic councils, they fought
because of memories of yellow stars,
of window glass crashing all around.
Warriors without weapons,
infantry with rusted rifles,
still they fought.
None of them really meant it
when they said "goodbye."

This year, again, sons and daughters
stand in this place struggling
not to see. Remembrance is costly.

Young women walk out, hair pulled
back and braided, faces soapy clean.
Young men, small caps clipped on,
unbearded, stride beside them.
Thigh muscles tighten and release;
fingertips tingle; mouths open;
hands fall ready to caress;
arms, to enfold, to feel their strength.

For a time they will fondle guns,
insert cartridges, rise sweating in
the night, hearts beating in time to
a marching rhythm.
Now the yellow stars have faded,
and the window glass no longer shatters down.

Councils of strategy avoid their searchlight eyes
and read them tales of David and of Solomon.
They float on a tide that ebbs and flows
from hope to despair because the augury
they rely on is interpreted by men.

The troops will march if Meir sends them.
Moshe can push their planes into the sky.
Aaron and Baruch will drop the bombs.
Anna and Sara will fire the rounds.
Riva and Avrom,
Itzak and Debra,
all now aim to slaughter,
deaf to screams.
Mercy has no place in the blood
sacrifice to an indifferent god.
Only victory is in their prayers.
None will really mean it
when they say "goodbye."

THE REFINERY

High, skeletal erector-set
towers, a small city, top-lit,
scattered points of light,
pipes, tubes swelling
into giant storage spheres
nested into metal collars,

empty into swollen hoses
        wheels turn
          gears mesh
gravity slides oil to level one.

Hard-hat wearers muscle around
tower bases, check valves, leaks.
Watchmen watch runners, climbers,
anyone who moves. Flames
shoot up chimneys, burn off
excess gas, slyly cheat the world.

Crude sludges through arteries
carried from killed fields
where mineral-soaked weeds
brown out in dry weather.
Deep below ground
a Mesozoic mix—decayed vegetation
and bones of extinct beasts
morphed into black pits.

Energy demands
exponential as population
multiplies
        never enough
        never enough.

No leisure to dwell
on philosophy

or the nature of man
        day shift
        night shift
        clock in
        clock out
fillers of the stomachs
of tankers
on water or land.

Predators watch, follow the slick,
to swallow the oil.
Greedy enough to kill,
to steal our black liquid,
our golden energy,
so much easier to pilfer
than the gold of the mines.

Some come from
countries far removed
from the western world
with accidental spills,
embarrassing destruction;
from the eastern world
where explosions incinerate
a dozen men at a time.

We are still here.
We stand firm.
We protect the oil.

THE SWIMMER

Crows, nature's flyover drones, land
and hop, arrogant in a search for insects,
croaking as they fly away when
the swimmer splashes out of the water.
She stands erect on the pool deck,
eyes sweeping over windows.

Body straight, face imperturbable,
she knows no grind of secret pain,
no dread of a future without joy.
Wrapped in embroidered robe,
she ascends to her room, removes
the scarlet swimsuit, kicks it away.

THE SCARLET SUIT

was sewn halfway around the world,
shipped to a top-label designer
in the cramped hold of a freighter
sailing from a third-world country
as impoverished as its citizens,
denizens of crumbling shacks,
scavengers for daily bread.

Women all but shackled to the bosses'
machines, seeing daughters struggle
as well, all the days, nights,
all the years for pennies, the blood
from fingers punctured by needles,
torn by rough threads will not
be visible on a scarlet suit.

THE THREE B'S

Bam, bam de bam

hands whap tight drum skins,
open palms slap kneecaps,
slap torsos on parade.

chunk a chunk chunk

netted shells scrape, drag
across hollow gourds
the shakera's
scattery rattle

IN MALI

bare feet pounded
into deep dust, knees bent
bodies leaned into drum-
beats, men squatted
by grounded djembes.

drowned by sweat,
flesh jiggling
women held gourds high

backs bending, rising,
they glanced over
a shoulder at a baby's
head bouncing
tied by a scarf
above mama's backside

IN LOS ANGELES

carpet-muffled
                 our shoes tap
one/two
whispery sizzle,
of brushes on cymbals
wah wild metallic trumpet
               gold bellow saxophone mouth
               hollow-cheeked sucked in electronic
wow,
               quivering sounds
of tomorrow
and now
shiver of electric bass
twang of acoustic guitar

smack of skin against skin
steady beat of feet
people pop up/
               down
vibrations hold us in thrall

to *bam, bam de bam*
to rhythm.

THE VIEW FROM ABOVE

LA to Boston

Earth's rotation is fixed,
the plane speeds opposite,
gazing down, crags and valleys
slide one into the next.
Mountain tops, white-sheeted or
gravelly-bare, bulk up into cloud
curtains that reveal through stringy
wisps the dark green blue of forests.

Bleach-boned deserts, thirsting
cacti, tumbleweeds
graduate into green growth,
watered into precise rows,
straight-furrowed with a circular
path of revolving
irrigation pipes mimicking Nazca
circles, without the alien mystery.

Suddenly canals, rivers and then
the mighty one slicing
the land from north to south.
Beyond, streets of houses,
Monopoly-sized with slanted
roofs, fringe the edges of black
asphalt swoops just before
the highway takes off, linking
towns like necklace beads.

We descend over hi-rises.
Landing wheels shudder into
place. I shudder with them,
uncertain who will be
there when we land.

THROAT SINGERS

Winter in a far north Inuit village is hushed,
sunless. Outside the igloo, work time, play
time is brutal, short. Inside, the only
electricity is a buzz between two people.

Holding each other's forearms, a couple
faces each other with open round mouths.
Making a small bellow, musical but hollow,
each directs the sound through the other's
mouth against the other's throat.

Sound bounces back and forth
reverberating, echoing, re-echoing
off the back of each throat,
pulsing through an invisible
tunnel from mouth to mouth.

Throat singers stand, practice
through long darkness,
letting each small bellow swell,
enthralled with melodic
rhythm, the feeling of ancient

voices anomalous in this
electronic time.

TOKYO FESTIVAL

Days beyond snowflakes and raindrops,
the baby dragon's breath gentles cherry
trees into pink blossoms, laid out into
pointillist comforters over the grass, under
branches knobby with half-petalled flowers.

Students pack up books. Secretaries
and their male bosses pour into jammed
subways, assume the popular position,
heads cocked, eyes closed, ignoring
standing elders, head for Ueno Park.

Eager friends on staked-out blue plastic
spaces fence them off with beer-filled
coolers, containers of fish cakes,
vinegared rice. In latticed light,
Japanese chat, anticipate with shining eyes.

Youths yell, wave cell phones, signal
their select group. Latecomers patch onto
sparser grass, bumpy with tree roots, relish
the spring festival until dark brings
piled plastics, overflowing cans.

Only the shoes, lined up with care,
form a neat fringe around the blue plastic
in respect for the temporary living space,
honor for the shared party carpet.

TOWERS OF SILENCE

"Burial of flesh corrupts the earth."
—*Zoroaster*

Once, huge birds spiraled down, spread
their feather-fingered wings, circled
until wailing mourners disappeared.

The vultures, when they landed,
lost all gracefulness,
scrabbled for balance on rocky ledges,
beaks poised above the corpse.
The body, freshly cleansed,
was tendered to the vultures
since the birds leave only bones.

After the Islamic revolution here, this
practice was proscribed. Now these two
towers of silence host the heat,
the desiccating winds, people curious
enough to climb the hill.

In the town of Yazd, nearby, the symbol
of Ahura Mazda fronts a temple, I see
where Zoroastrians worship light
emitted from a fire they claim
has burned three hundred years.

The mullahs, ayatollahs let them stay,
but many of the Parsees moved abroad.
Some to Bombay. There are many there.
Some, I met here, live in California now.

Still I see, high in Iranian skies,
the vultures sailing in circles
while they watch and wait.

TWO AFRICAS

A hut interior so dark,
the family group melded
black on black, receding
into darkness, away from photos.
I hold a basket, grass- and fiber-
woven with a top, cowrie shells
decorate the base. Lift the cover,
a waft of African dust puffs out.
A light gasp from the past.

Black clay flask, oil container,
its round bottom inside a woven,
contoured base. Wooden carvings,
human figures, roughly done or highly
finished, pride of workmanship
evident in one special figure.

Creations direct from the artist,
from a shop in Addis, or Bamako,
or from a peddler's cart outside of Abidjan.
For me, memories. For the creators,
crafts made for tourist dollars,
help in survival,

to stay alive, were created in moments
stolen from gleaning of sparse fields,
digging desiccated roots to roast,
lugging water in from drying village wells,
pounding millet into mealie.

I could have eased family burdens,
saved a child, fed an elder, allowed
tribesmen, tribeswomen a chance
to move forward, less need to beg
for food on crowded city streets.

VENUS' FLOWER

After months on a ship,
enveloped by bluster
and testosterone,
where the feel of a woman
was a feature of dreams,
they walked on ground again,
bodies reeled to the pitch
of the waves, minds drunk
on memories of sweethearts,
wives, even pock-marked faces
of whores on the streets of Cadiz.

This flower, so exotic,
unlike any known,
with purple-red lips
engorged as with blood,
smelled so seductive
to ants and to flies,
they thought—woman.
Her attraction to men,
her amazing behavior.

Watching the plant
devour its insects,
longing to be
consumed by a woman,
they named the flower
after a goddess of love.

Drawn to beckoning tendrils,
awed by danger in its beauty,
caught in Aphrodite's mousetrap,
they conquered the sisters,
wives, daughters of natives
discovered in this new world.

WEDDING GUEST

I watch the people proceed
as the groom, in ivory turban
with a cockade and a jewel,
rides a white horse, dismounts
to join the bride in a gold-threaded
sari beneath a canopy of scarlet,
fringed with orange pompoms.
Vibrant, glowing bride
and groom exude an aura
of expectancy and hope.

Women, one nostril pierced
with a sparkling stud, wear
bracelets from wrist to elbow,
send a shiver of silver
as they wave their arms, spin.
Hindu blessings, godly prayers,
are promises enough to send
the couple, the crowd, witnesses
to the joining, off to celebrate,
drink, eat, dance, enjoy.

The throng rushes off,
leaving me. I turn,
feel compelled to chase
after them, turn back,
face an empty street
littered with torn,
trampled bits of gilded
paper, shining foil. Dancers,
musicians, all vanished.

I run up and down nearby
alleys, frantic, searching,
find no celebration,
no other wedding guest.

WITHIN THE CIRCLE

The monotony of deep-voiced
chants suits my somber mood.
The folds of their dark orange robes
flash scarlet when they move.
Their shaved heads are smooth,
reflect the light from a single bulb.

The minutiae of the task are daunting
and tension grows among those of us
who watch from the shadows, despite
the calm of the Tantric Buddhist monks
as they make the mandala of sand,
placing only a few grains at a time.

The ritual honors Yamantaka, a deity
whose body parts stand for truth,
for enlightenment, and for the emptiness
of all concerns of the worldly mind.

Groups of four young monks
and an elder rotate for three full days.
At the end of the third day,
they destroy all of their work.

The pains they took, the beauty,
the pure meditation,
these are their goals.

I study the monks, leave
for a while, come back
to sit alone in the shadows,
surrounded by chanting,
repetitive and hypnotic,
a sponge for weariness.

I feel their compassion
as they reach out to me
from within the circle.

WORLDEATER

Gonzo, scribbling nibbler, tasting his way around the world

      herring rollmops,
      bratwurst, sauerkraut
      paella, tapas
      tajines, jollof rice
      carne barbacoa
      samosas, tandoori, naan
      udon, chow fun, pancit
      burgers, fries
      hummus, pomegranates

finds a new Middle Eastern cuisine
                meals ready to eat
                        blackened by bursting shells
                              seasoned with shrapnel
             al fresco dining.

YIJIH-SHIN

The golden lady Buddha statue
rises three stories high.
Below—grotesque, dome-headed
dwarves, craggy-featured,
posture among trees.
Yijih-Shin, lady monk
here at Fo Guang Shan,

meets us to watch
marching lines of foreign students,
monastic or lay or local Taiwanese,
file past into a cavernous hall.
They sit, chant to the Buddha
as bowls are filled, then
they eat in silence.

Yijih-Shin led us
to a small square-cornered
room, all grays, beiges, neutral
as her loose brown robe. Her
shaved head shone, polished.
Seated across, she stared at me
with light, prominent eyes.

She, resident here for thirty
years, was enthusiastic about
her satisfying existence without
possessions, a fulfilled life dedicated
to study, Buddhist discipline,
prayers, and pride in her
monastery's aid to disaster

victims, the homeless, the starving.
Lunch served, her focus
changed to complete consumption.

Her eyes bulged as she ate,
head bent over her full bowl,
spoon ceaseless as a machine.
She emptied her bowl,

eyed several side dishes
remaining unfinished,
gobbled them up and anything
uneaten. Our small group
of international travelers

sat in silence and wonder
while workers removed

empty dishes, never
looking at her, seeming
unruffled by her frenzy.
At last she stopped,
sat erect, at ease, her
eyes refocused.
She burped politely,

led us out, expressed
pleasure at hosting us, invited
us to revisit, as manners
require in Taiwanese culture.
We shared looks and nodded,
still appalled by her voracious
appetite. Frightening.

She had such need to fill
some aching void, an emptiness
belying her words of contentment.
Replete now, she relaxed.
Her smile widened. Beneath
her ample robe she seemed
to have grown softly larger.

FIRST PAIN

On a hut's dirt floor, the village midwife uses lore and herbs.
City sidewalks don't nurture birthing, so women go where
a washed pale green softens the starched tunics of doctors,
nurses, the hard finish of sheets cast over bent legs.

Her face twists as regular, rhythmic, intense muscles
stretch her womb's mouth into a grimace, a mirror of her rictus.
Dilations, snail-paced, concede one centimeter at a time.

> Nurse mantra one: *breatheinexpanddontpushbreatheout*
> *breatheinexpanddontpushbreatheout.*

White-knuckled, she squeezes railings, writhes in our arms. I breathe
with her, will her thrashing to slow, for her to draw strength from our
strength. Gasping, cries rising, her womb's flesh stretches wider, wider.

> Nurse mantra two: *breatheholdpushagainpush*
> *breatheholdpushagainpush.*

Curling over her child, grabbing her knees, she bears down. Nurses cheer
her on. I join in as assistant coach, count onetwothreefour . . .
  breathe, start
over. She curses the world, god, men who trap women into this torture.

> Nurse mantra three: *hereitcomespushharderharder*
> *hereitcomespushharderharder.*

I stand amazed; flesh and blood, dark curls like wet feathers, crowning cap.
Doctor hands fasten on the newborn head, pull, twist shoulders, boy-child
plunges face out into open air. Leaving his sealed, airless, sunless bath
for the only time, his mother for the first time.

Child-star lifted aloft, well and truly born. The new mother wails,
confused after her injuries, sewn up, blood washed from body, wall
  and floor.
first pain ended—she knows not all pain caused by this child is finished.

70

HOMECOMING

Tendrils of fog,
those ragged remnants that soak up
the rain, intensify the sun's rays.
Focused by the window's
beveled edges, they fill
my eyes with too much
light and make them tear.

I watch the jet engine,
its gray hump part of one
slanted wing. Flaps move,
ready for descent.

I visualize arrival gates,
lounges, waiting people:
a man with flowers
to give to his lover,
a guide with a sign,
a welcome for a stranger,
an infant held high
so that grandma sees him first.

I know there won't
be anyone who's come
there just for me.

I already miss the friends
who had touched me
with their kindness, made
me feel wanted. More than
their culture or manners,
I felt they really cared.

We had shared blankets spread
under cherry trees, looked
up at the sky through pink or white
flowers, enjoyed a picnic supper.

At a ryokan, all of us women,
sitting in steaming tubs,
speaking different languages,
splashed each other and smiled.

Now, the plane speeds me
toward reality; that other world
part of a memory
already misplaced.

II
Here We Live Forever
Family

CLOWNS

with bulbous noses, like W.C. Fields,
swaggered like drunks. I eyed one,
striped socks flecked with sawdust,
waving floppy flowers. Lifted
eyebrows, bright red triangles
Satanic over dark-lined eyes,
dripped mascara into faux
tears. They were not in pain.

With wanton gestures, they caressed
each other's ballooning breasts.
Exploding firecrackers, puffs of smoke,
and clowns climbed over each other,
mounted swaying ladders. They raised
full skirts over bulging pantaloons
while air horns burped. I cowered

when they chased each other into
the circus stands, embarrassed
by their lack of self-control.
Other children, families howled
with laughter, but, afraid of clowns
poking fun at my crimson face,

I hid against my father's chest,
trusting, without words,
he would understand my fear,
protect me, always.

DINNER HOUR

She was penny-wise,
shopped discretely,
cooked with caution,
seasoned sparely.

The kitchen was her bastion,
the family, her only legion,
hers to serve. At six p.m.
the gates clanged shut,
a minute later she would
pace, *tut tut* at the pots,
as though to slow their boiling,
rescue dinner for a little while.

A long work day, a school delay
was no excuse. Atonement
filled the hours between meals.

I rushed in, losing to the clock,
to face the hurt, accusing look.
I swallowed my day's
accomplishment, excitement
held it all inside—
my throat too tight,
my voice too small
to overcome the silence.

EXCURSION: 1948

Butcher shop
red meat glistened, grained
by cream-colored fat,
punctured by bone bits. Chosen
cuts removed to a thick
wood-block table, chopped,
wrapped, laid on the cold
marble countertop.

Bakery
smells from hot ovens,
delicious inhalation,
poppy seed coffee cake,
a whole rye loaf
sliced with one motion
into sandwich sized sections.

Grocery
cabbages, piles
of winter pears, summer peaches,
each piece squeezed,
pinched, picked, bagged,
tossed with the rest
into a carry sack.

People
best of all
and not family.
I stared, they watched me,
spoke to me, smiling
as strangers do
when they meet a child's eyes.

TRUE STORY

When my mother
thrust me into my room,
ordering me not
to be a nuisance,
she never knew
I was really a princess
strangely estranged
from my respectful,
adoring subjects,
misplaced in a family,
so different from me.

SCOREKEEPER

Spotlights splay out light rays, gritty
with moth flakes burned from wings
that brushed too close to a bulb.
The light discourages team uniforms
into even grayer dinginess darkened
by underarm shadows of male sweat,
livened a little bit by the logo of
the Hollywood Stars outlined in blue.

Bang! Another foul ball rattles the
metal screen behind home base that
protects foolish rooters from fouls
and the field from the foolish rooters.
The noise sounds like the thunder
imitations made by radio sound men
when they undulate corrugated tin.

Thud! A wooden bat hits home plate as
another batter steps up to do the ritual:
the bat bang
the foot swivel
the spit onto dirt
the shift of chaw in mouth
the rubbing of hands with earth.
This player bellies up, stomach
overhanging the too tight elastic
band at this waist. He's the Babe,
from the minors long ago, but
still monikered the Babe.

Ump's fingers up, ump's fingers down,
his arms wipe an imaginary cleanup.
This guy's not going to hit anything
tonight—again—still he's in the lineup.

Easy for me. I don't have to mark down
anything much. Just another K on the page.
I have plenty of other notes though:
one-bagger
three-bagger
walk
bunt
sacrifice
error
numbers of the ball throws, who made plays.

This is my job. This is why I am here.
He knows I'm not a boy,
but he damn sure won't
admit I'm a girl. I don't
realize it myself, so I come.
I sit, like a too-round pea
in my seat pod, invisible to
everyone, even my father.

Treat for me—the peanut vendor
comes and with his overhand pitch
casts the cheap paper packages,
red-striped, down the aisles, and I
get to eat, cracking the nuts, throwing
shells and nut skins on the ground
to mound among empty paper cups.
I get a hot dog—delicious, mustardy,
dripping on my hand and the score
card. I am distracted by the food,
the screams of fans yelling at the ump,
yelling at the other team. My father
hollers at me, "Keep score. Keep score."

The game ends, my job is finished.
"Let's go, it's late, hurry up now."
He doesn't take my hand, but he
grabs the scorecard, scans it, and
I see it fall, to land among the
discards on the stadium steps.

FAMILY VACATION

My body, wedged between two boulders,
is invisible to walkers puffing uphill
from Avalon. An edge of my mind
focuses on sails slicing across the bay
as I gather words for a story

about an athletic girl who hits
the softball every time at bat,
kills a shot over the volleyball
net, and never flubs a serve.
She is fought over, chosen first

by all the teams. My parents,
sister are specks on the beach.
I'd rather sit alone, grow my
words like mollusks inside thick
shells, my armor against my family's

grins and teasing when they mock
my writing. I choose a pen name,
write a poem about a girl
who discovers she is really a princess,
beloved, countrywide, by friends

and strangers. The carillon chimes
behind me: I am expected at the beach.
I stall to compose a song for piano and
voice to be sung to an eager audience.
Any vacation, even the annual one

on this island with my family, frees
me from my real world. I must go back
to the search for someone to share lunch
or a movie matinee and wait to be invited
to somebody's home for a sleepover.

McGUFFEY ANN

Under tree boughs sweeping over wrappings sprinkled
with a confetti of green needles, I found my special gift
my nine-year-old heart had longed for her, the only doll
I ever, ever really wanted in the whole world. My father

had fulfilled my wish, he usually did, mother complied.
I tore off white ribbon, blue wrappings, there she was.
Two braids, the color of straw and just as stiff,
under a woven hat with a scalloped rim, a plaid ribbon

around the crown, matching dress of blue, red, green,
over it a white pinafore, like one my aunt sewed for me.
I lifted her, her blue eyes opened, my most beautiful
doll. Her skin was creamy, smooth, cool, a perfect

WASP, confident, self-assured, all that I was not. Other
gifts forgotten, I recall the pine smell of the Chanukah bush,
my parents' annual attempt to function like a solid, healthy
family, be like everyone else—not Jewish, not different.

Years after I had grown up, given my dolls away, I left too. My father
was shamed before his friends, a daughter only left her family
for marriage. He died young, without me there. I remember
the day I got McGuffey Ann and his big smile at my happiness.

STAMP COLLECTION

I fitted each stamp by a hinge,
thin as a cell, into a black outline.

My fingertips tingled at embossed
blue, purple birds of paradise,

mountains in Azerbaijan, Tannu
Tuva outlined on triangle shapes.

Hyenas, leopards stalk through
dreamscapes by honored artists,

poets, composers, philosophers,
even kings portrayed, respected.

A dictator wearing a brush
moustache—despised, powerful.

My father took me to buy
stamps, or trade. Knowing

all about barter, business,
he felt at ease there

where my needs were easy
to fathom, easy to fulfill.

MOTHER'S DAY

It was round, a ceramic candy box
with an elf dressed in green tights
and a tunic perched on the lid.
Its pale, glazed face had a turned-up nose
and a mocking smile, and it wore its pink floppy hat
at a careless, rakish angle.
The elf had a mischievous presence
as it sat among spotted mushrooms
and a few spikes of grass.

When I first saw the box
in a gift shop window,
so graceful and delicate, I knew
I had to buy it for my mother.
It took all the money I'd saved
from my allowance. I brought
it home, wrapped it clumsily.

I gave it to her with great
anticipation. Perhaps,
I could make her happy.

She unwrapped it, opened the lid,
and glanced inside. In silence,
she replaced the lid.
As she rewrapped the box
and pulled the bow tight,
our eyes met, and then,
she looked away.

A PARALLEL UNIVERSE

He chose me, moved me into
adult times—jazz clubs, furtive weekends.
High school bodice-rippers portrayed
breathless love as wearing out,
ending with marriage vows. We
took them anyway, legally done,
new homes, travel, many parties,
too much booze. The scent of
bodies aged, altered, we stayed
together until we didn't.

Time: endings began, a death,
a new love, another death,
smaller place, night memories,
I follow the strings—go back,
holes in space, replace
regretted words, change history—
in this parallel universe.

I want it again, living with
whatever love I had,
sharing life, backwards running
film is false. I want it
even though ghosts of dead cannot rise
nor can the dead themselves.
Still . . .

REMEMBERING

Blindness is an isolating state.
He did not want pity, had known
for years that childhood
diabetics can lose their sight.
My cousin had seen my face
once or twice since his marriage.

His talking clock, books on tape,
vocal alarms impressed my teenage
mind. More than amusements,
they were really, truly needed.
Their house stood out
with its radio tower looming

over neighboring roofs. They
traveled the world, seeing
foreign countries vicariously
through other eyes, speaking "radio-ese"
or pidgin English, swapping

local, colorful stories.
Earthquakes, floods, fires
exploded, and victims, frantic
to reach family and friends,
did so through ham to ham
connections. Proud of their

role, he and his wife gave
life-affirming support during
widespread catastrophes.
A slow recovery from
amputation of a leg, unable
to visit, we spoke on the phone.

I cannot forget his last words,
in my mind you will always be sixteen.

BIRTHDAY DINNER

They met at an upscale restaurant. Popular but pricey. Cost had never been a factor for him when it came to eating out. He arrived first, as she had planned.

She was wearing an expensive new dress, certain he would be aware of that—he knew women's clothes, used to shop with her. Helping her choose had made him less critical of her appearance. Tonight, she wore makeup, something fairly new for her.

She was thinner, had almost given up food for the past month. He looked the same as always, well-groomed, possibly wearing a new shirt and tie, she wasn't sure.

His greeting was cool and subdued as she joined him. It had been agreed beforehand that there would be no scenes—it was a public place. No yelling. No tears.

She ordered the most expensive entrée, appetizer, good wine, wanting to make him pay.

They talked about children, a grandchild, what they were up to recently. She didn't hear a word after he mentioned that he was going on a trip. He would be traveling with a companion. She had made no travel plans.

With a dry mouth, she asked why he was taking her out to dinner?
He said it was his birthday.
She knew that. What was the real reason?
He hoped she would be understanding, make it easy on them both, see their accountant to help make a fair settlement, go easy on lawyers' fees.
Her mouth fell open, but there was nothing to say.

Everything around her suddenly stood out, sharp and clear
        as though it had to be memorized.
The wine looked exceptionally red, a beautiful, deep color. The

glasses, sparkling crystal, reflected the light from the chandeliers. The linen was peach-colored. The flowers on the table were fresh roses and carnations. The room was filled; most were couples. Each person, softly lit, sat smiling and silent.

She could not hear conversations nor any other sound. Mirrors on both sides of the room reflected images across to each other, back and forth.

CONSUMMATION

Perhaps you came to bed
wearing your watch
to measure the dream's finish,
when it would run its course, no longer
recurrent, the idyll's end,
the fable's demise,
the end of joining privately,
lying exposed, should anyone
else in this or any universe
second guess our pastime
on afternoons when spouses
played enthralled at timeless
occupations, when we,
unwatched, held ourselves
bound only to each other,
immersed in sharing minds,
and other intimate favors,
until minutes dissolved, hours
devoured, we withdrew from
deep-plumbed folds
holding no unknowns but one,
that one, once detected,
caught you in a web of pain,
swept love of life over love of love
when, all regret, apology,
you abandoned my bed
to struggle long,
lose at last, lie consigned,
concealed, unforgiven
in a box consumed by fire.

DRINKING SONG

Here's to the uncles with pot bellies flowing,
an expanse of ribs and ripples, dotted
with follicles. The pale belly
is unshrinking from the sun, shining
its fire on oiled skin, coloring it through
the spectrum of colors, beginning with pink.

Here's to nieces, bare breasts quivering, moving
with catlike stretches, indolent yawns,
lengthening her limbs along the beach lounge,
while dark nipples rise to the pinch of uncle's
fingers, his caress of thong-outlined thighs.
A fair exchange for five-star luxury.

Here's to the aunts, residing up north,
wrapped in woolens, dozing before a fire,
relishing uncle's absence, relief from
less pleasant wifely duties, smiling
at the stories he will tell about his work
week reluctantly spent in Greece.

EULOGY

My small family of five was placed behind a gauzy curtain,
        separated from three others who were there,
        presumably so we could weep in peace.

The rabbi parroted what he'd been told an hour earlier:
        my mother had loved to shop,
        to see her grandkids—
        he didn't know that I had made them visit
        with me, so I didn't have to go alone.

My oldest son had asked to give a eulogy.
        He spoke about her reading books to him
        and playing ball when he was small.
        She had told him she gave out mail in the home,
        talked about the bingo games, the crafts she made,
        her favorite TV programs and the ones she didn't like.

He had written this and never told us
        what he'd planned to say. He made us
        feel that he would miss her: he had cared.

We were astonished,
        thanked him for his words.

I felt hollow, dismayed.
        I must have been there
        when they spoke
        and never heard a thing.

She hadn't shared the content
        of her days with me,
        and I had never asked.

FIFTH COMMANDMENT

Inside the chapel,
light, diffuse as thought,
emanates from sconces
placed so as not to throw
a shadow. Respectful black
shapes the company
into mourners.
One eulogy reaches me
with high school memories.
I think about renewing
friendships in later years
and something else.

I puzzle over an almost
recalled moment that slithers
away just as I could capture it.
I follow other mourners out,
stare at trees, the valley view,
green slopes, manicured plots.
As I walk away it hits me
with a wrench of disbelief:
my father and mother, both,
are buried on this very hill.

GEORGE

He planted flowers, weeded,
fertilized, catered to the seasons,
buried stalks for rains to cry over

                    We cut the blooms.

Satsuma came, too, his daughter
with the name like a plum,
petite, round, with straight,
shiny black hair

                    Dolls spoke for us.

George gave us beautiful, exotic gifts:
a pair of badminton paddles,
upholstered with red and gold faux
brocade, one was a geisha woman,
the other a samurai man. In a glass case,
a graceful statue, fan held in delicate
hands, feet angled in a dance, had
the other-worldly face of a Hokusai lady.

                    We put them away on a shelf.

The day George went away, his old truck
was parked in our garage with lawn mower,
edgers, clippers, sealed boxes surrounding it.
He left his keys; everything he owned
was in our care.

                    He had no one to trust but us.

My father moved the truck each week.
Everything else was left as it was.
Without being sure, my father guessed
George would be gone a long time.
He sent a card or two, at the beginning.

                    He was gone for three years.

The day George returned, he claimed his
equipment, went away from us and from
Los Angeles. Feelings of friendship dried up
in the desiccating winds of Manzanar.
Living in wooden barracks, sand sifting
in through slats and shingles had buried

his caring with his pride.
His family, living only with Japanese,
communicating in Japanese.

They decided they preferred it that way.
"But why leave us," I said.
"We didn't do anything."

"We didn't do *anything*."

HOLES

Open guts of a mountain,
exposed bowels of coal
excreted into railroad cars,
trucked across innocent deserts,
burned for power to placate
citizens with bottomless need.

Smaller holes, plugs of dirt,
planted beds of tulips, tomatoes.
Larger, deeper ones, filled
with fruit trees or solid
sycamores for nesting
birds, climbing animals,
scraped-knee children.

Temporary holes in dunes or flat
beach sands, sliding, filling
as soon as they are dug.
Youngsters try to core the earth,
dig to China. Nicolas,[1] buried,
jumps up, scattering sand grains
into his nose, mouth.

Silent interior holes.
Closets without clothes,
beds without occupants,
no cook in the kitchen,
no hand on a doorknob,
no voice in any room,
no music.

---

1   Joyce's grandson

INTERIORS

Clothes on hangers offer sterile shapes.
The contours, the faint smell of aftershave
come from the man who wears them.

His few tailored suits, dark blue or gray,
are de rigueur for Monday–Thursday wear
(jeans, okay for casual Fridays,
have no holes or fraying hems).

With dress shirts, thin-striped or solid colors,
he coordinates silk ties all with diagonal bands
like the ones his father wore.

Shelves hold folded sweats, T-shirts worn to advertise
the pecs he develops from his daily workouts.

      In the back,
separated from the rest,
are tight black leather trousers
and a matching jacket.
Supple, shaped to fit his frame,
they flaunt a polished gleam and silver buttons,
designed to reflect the scattered light
in the interiors of darkened bars.

JUDGMENT

Her head scarf slips down
below her chin, tightens—
a noose or a warning.
Shadows creep.

Walk between daylight and
dark and tongues will wag,
bid males to rush home,
rescue family honor, ensure
the purity of the female bait
necessary to entice suitable
suitors, fix an agreeable price—
dowry for family coffers.

I, too, made a choice, but
it was my choice, not
my family's. I sold myself
too young, fearful of natural
needs, urges, of strengthening
desire, of invoking the
goddess of fertility,
for protection against my
version of wagging tongues.

Some alternatives are too
risky, better to face my
critical self at a later date,
me the only judge.

HONEYMOON ...

Tasting time, different salt
for different flesh, darker,
maybe, or pinker,
before the first
confusion, the fresh physique.

Smells need a chance
to be absorbed, reconciled.
Each secret orifice produces
an odor to be fathomed
by the new partner.

A sound on an adjacent
pillow, startling, unexpected
breath in a waxy ear,
exhales, body contractions.

Protrusions, hollows,
clefts, hair in natural
places, roughness revealed
without foundation makeup,
without the razor's action.

Shared space, depleted grace,
chores, obligations, forces,
deficiencies rise to critical points.

I thought. He thought.
We didn't expect
so many leftover bumps,
so many years to overcome
and we—
didn't have the patience.

LOST INNOCENCE

Rows of houses, full stuccoed, cast shadows, a fraction
darker than the asphalt, black against stippled gray

with roofs—hard triangles, as in a child's
drawing—implying, as the two-dimensioned world

of children does, that all imagined residents
are flat as well, living within rectangular shapes,

people flattened by sickness, betrayal by trusted
ones, near or far, by promises their leaders

spout as freely as water gushes up, blown out
from whale spouts, gaining force from hard blowing.

LOU

She rode the bus for an hour and a half
from South Central to Silver Lake.
In a neat yellow blouse
and dark skirt she trudged uphill
to find me wearing sweats.

She brought sparkles with her, smiled
at me and my three little boys, managed
to work around the mess, gave me
precious time to shop alone.
The sparkle lasted almost all week long.

We talked—her son, a casualty
of Vietnam, a metal plate inserted
in his skull, had recurring nightmares
that sometimes screamed him
into the VA hospital, letting her
keep some sanity and her jobs.
I never told her I hated the war,
demonstrated, marched down
Wilshire Boulevard with my kids in tow.

At her daughter's wedding—my first
in an African Methodist Church—she
beamed at the bride in white, bridesmaids
in yellow chiffon, her son in a tuxedo.
She wore plain, matronly blue.

Sometimes her husband, grizzled, aging,
dressed in a worn suit, drove her to work
on his way to his trash-collecting job.
He drove a four-door Chevy, the hood
was locked with a chain around
the front bumper. They had to park
it outside, in front of their house.

The night the Watts riots hit Los Angeles
she called in terror. Their local grocery
burned out, a police cordon around
their neighborhood, they had no food.
My husband threw our freezer
contents into plastic bags, made a plan
to meet, drove down himself, alone.
I protested—he would put himself,
all of us, in danger. He went anyway.

He was right, but I never told him
I admired him for his courage.

After the fires died and the buses
ran again, Lou came back.
We never spoke about the riots,
burned-out buildings, lost jobs,
or the anguish of her family.

She followed when we moved
even farther from her home.
My wise adviser through spiking
fevers, past broken arms, even
into my too-frequent spousal spats,
she stayed until her husband's
cancer forced her to retire.

I looked for her years later,
checked with other families,
she'd left them all. I called
the only number I had left.
A woman, suspicious, answered,
asked me who I was and what I
wanted, then denied that she
had ever heard of Lou.

From my sheltered circle,
I tried to reach out to the world
in which she lived or used to live.
I was not allowed to touch
her life again.

MOMHOOD

His loss of a job is my loss, too.
When he suffers his divorce,
I remember the pain, the split
from his father.

His request for help is joined
with an apology. He wants
me to still be mom,
the den mother,
carpool driver,
school volunteer,
caretaker I used to be,

The task he calls me
to is no longer mine.
It should be his.
Our separate roles
are topsy-turvy now.

PHOTOS OF MY CHILDREN

demystify the partial
recollections I recycle.
I listened too well,
never strained knowledge
through a sieve to pick out
good parts, discard
shells and pods.

I have no memory of so much smiling,
still vague about their teenage troubles.
They reached beyond my grasp,
repressed their trepidation,
disbelief in any grown-up
who clothed the truth, forced
sparse conversation,
queries remained unasked.

Framed, cardboard spines
hold them up, stand them tall.
Glass, dear Glass, protect them from evil,
erosion of strength. Guarded,
as they once were,
they will not change nor be changed.

Here we live forever.
Wilde misunderstood,
it is the image that must stay the same,
fixed within the frame.

Turned to the wall,
they were never born at all.

FOUND/LOST

Almost awake, I stare,
aghast, at my vertical
window blinds, squint
as my husband's face,
an apparition, splits
into long puzzle pieces,
nose on one slat, one eye
each on two others,
his full-lipped mouth
spread across several.

A moment passes,
a strange wind disturbs
the slats, splinters his
features into separate
strips, dissolves
them into broken lines,
like a pencil sketch
slow to be erased.

ON LEAVING LOS ANGELES

The fragile bit of near-translucent
flesh is expelled from my womb.
I flush it down, start its journey
to the ocean through
sewers, wide cement caverns,
sloshing with other discarded

life—goldfish released
to head for Alaska, chicks
smothered by excess love
of little Easter celebrants.

They weep for their loss.
My sorrow wears away,
follows the travels
of the unborn with wishes—

Be glad to go down
into the sewers. Escape
a world where
you are not welcome.

Leave behind the wrecks
of ships with gold that
will not be spent,
the purse seines rotting,
tangled up with bones
of fishermen and dolphins.
Descend to the cold
depths where no rays
penetrate so blindness
has no meaning.
Sink into the cloying
sand that will cover
you with blankets,
the burial
I could not give.

OTHERS

were not family—she feared
them, even those she saw
daily, grocery shopping

could deceive us, an accepted
invitation obligated her, in turn,
to ask them over to our house

could not be trusted, girls
my age might seek to be
my friend and then abandon me

envied us our solid family,
could steal my mother's time,
make her neglect her home

were the ones unfairly left intact
after all her sisters died,
her husband crippled by a stroke

were the neighbors who protested
when she wandered into backyards
stared at them through windows

were doctors, one psychiatrist
who used electric shock, which
made her face look vacuous and tan

were hospital staff who told me,
after my father died, she was now
as competent as she would ever be.

FOR JACKIE, FROM JOYCE

It's not about
a home built over rocks
above the ocean,
or a summer
camp on a river,
or a red convertible.

It's about a twinkle,
a twisted eyebrow,
a shameless pun,
the people things
that a man
takes away with him,
leaving us the kernel
of who he was
for us to relish
in our own time.

Perhaps one day,
a child will say
to a pal,
"I have a funny
fish story to tell
you; it's about my
great-great-grandfather.
His name was Bill."

EXPATRIATES

They came from Kiev, the city with the great gate
that held off the conquerors; the city that never
forgave its citizens for being what they were; that
cast them into ghettoes; that refused to let them
control their destinies; that forbade them to walk
with their neighbors at night; that spat on them when
they walked, hatted, in their prayer shawls on the Sabbath.

They came from a city of onion domes, of one of the
three lavras in Russia/Ukraine where the monks
buried their dead in caves and continued to worship
along with them. The shriveled black skins were
wrapped in embroidered satin vestments that
sometimes revealed their desiccated fingers,
gnarled like roots and, like roots, buried underground.
The monks were more beloved than living men.

They came from a city of huge statues with ugly faces
that glowered over the city, holding swords that could
not strike in time. Later, another statue of entwined figures,
rough and black, sculpted the tortured, twisted limbs of
a hundred thousand people who were massacred and
buried there at Babi Yar. Plaques in three languages remember
the dead, but the visitors are not current residents of the city.

They came from the city where the Neva runs into the sea, and
they tripped over the rats as they ran to the few ships that
might save them, that might hold them and the relics they could
carry from abandoned lives. Their neighbors watched, and when
they had gone, rushed to see what they could glean for themselves
from the derelict buildings.

They went to places where they were not welcomed with open arms,
where they were spat upon as they walked, hatted, in their prayer
shawls on the Sabbath. They remembered well. Now they were able to:
forge their own chains,

make their own prisons,
build their own ghettoes.

MISSING

From Kiev, bouncing hard over rough seas, my grandfather, his
    wife, and infant son
(my father) came through Ellisgate to Pittsburgh. I used to study
    photographs of him, scratchy black and white ones, searching
    for my father's features in his face. No resemblance there, but I
    thought I would have liked to know him, nice to have a grandpa.

        I knew her well, my mother's mom. She lived with us. In
            her Liverpudlian
        accent, she sang childhood songs, quiet-voiced until she
            yelled at any stray
        dog that dared to visit our front lawn. She smelled of
            lavender and ginger.
        In her eighties she died. Not allowed to go to her funeral,
            I was confused
        about what happened to people when they died.

My father, bright beyond his education, competitive chess player,
    family man, he was
broken up when I moved out to find my own place. An
    entrepreneur generous to his
daughters, he bought us anything we wanted. Dead at 58 from self-
    neglect, cheated on his
diabetic diet. The past repeats. My sons knew him as a photograph,
    searched for a
resemblance to me or them.

        Mother never spoke of him, even when I dragged my
            kids to visit her. An
        incomplete personality (a psychiatrist said), she
            rebounded from a mental
        breakdown, lived a semi-independent life. In her
            seventies when she died
        (she lied about her age all her life), an autopsy concluded
            she decided
        it was time to die, and she did.

My husband, educated, active, traveled with me to many countries
   in Europe, partly
for corporate business, until he had a massive stroke, lived for years
   a hospital life.
His mind's clock stopped at 60, his heart much later. He confused
   his sons with his
Grandchildren, who knew him as a skeletal man in a bed or a
   wheelchair. The youngest
feared his unintelligible words and twisted thoughts.

   Grandfathers went missing for three generations. But,
      hey, remember me?
   I'm following the women's path, still here, fighting,
      arguing, traveling, holding my own, hoping for the
      best for my family in particular, the world in general,
   a poet who revels in life.

GRANDMOTHER

The house still stands, a faded chartreuse now
instead of stained white stucco. California wonder!
It was not torn down or drastically remodeled, so
the red-tiled roof, the square-columned
porte cochère, the narrow front porch, all remain.

My grandmother sat and rocked on that porch,
wearing a fine hair net, a gray match for her hair,
a flowered dress of some dark background,
heavy stockings, and comfortable oxfords.
She peered at the neighbors through rimless
glasses, rarely speaking, concentrating on her
enemy. She watched for any dog who dared to
set its paw on our front lawn. Mistrusting its
intentions, she was off the porch and after it
shaking her cane until it slunk away
confused, not understanding its transgression.

Like the dog, I never understood what I had done,
why she did not take me on her lap to rock along with her,
never hugged me close to her full chest or
kissed my cheek. She did not tell me stories of her
girlhood growing up in Liverpool, or of her husband
dead for many years before my birth, or the children
she had lost, the ones I did not know and never met.
I did not hear of how she came to cross the ocean
bringing household goods and older children.
My sister told me later how she sang to us,
but I remember nothing about that.
The songs in my head had a different source.

There was a day she fell and hit her head: I saw
the bruises on her forehead and her bloodied chin.
I felt excitement, danced around and called out,
"Maybe she is dead, could she be dead?"
I felt an intense interest, curiosity but no concern.

My father, angry, banished me inside, looked
after her, and in his fear forgot to tell me what
it was that I had done.
A long time after that she died, and I did not
attend her funeral. No one talked to me
about it. I stayed home and wondered why.
Her death took little color from my life, only
a dim gray presence that had disappeared.
The rocking chair had vanished from the porch.

EVA UNGER BERNSTEIN

In her small annex off our rumpus room,
she husbanded her treasures: crystallized
ginger, apricot brandy, and the powder
she dabbed on the face that had been
nourished by the damp climate of Liverpool.
She wore flowered dresses, laced up,
sturdy oxfords, and hair nets of a nylon
webbing, delicate, spidery, and gray.

Over a hundred years ago, Eva and Morris
brought seven little children to America,
to Chicago where, there, more were born,
and where my grandfather died. They
carried important things: some jewelry,
a set of Haviland china packed into
padded cases, memories that faded and
were not shared with me. There were
rumors of relatives gone to exotic places,
Kimberley, South Africa, others unremembered.

She sang English songs, a few German ones,
that were rocked into my ears as she held
me on her lap. She was Jewish, Hellenized,
spoke not a word of Yiddish, was not
religious. Her traditions were her own.
Some grandmas on our street had come
from Eastern Europe. Their homes had
different smells and different foods, and
they used words I didn't understand.
She taught me my first words, and I aped
them in the accent she brought with her.
Her strength was harder to imitate.

Her sturdiness, her strength of will had
been used up as the demands grew. My
two aunts, Sarah and Bertha, were older

and knew the world, were educated to
survive, had some of her traits; but some
of the others, especially her sons, had come
into less and less of the power she had
needed to bring a family across the ocean.
She bequeathed less and less to each
child as it came, and there were ten.
My mother was the youngest, and by the
time she was born, there was little of Eva's
understanding and vitality to be inherited.
My mother was an attenuated female
silhouette, full of holes like a lace collar,
lacking substance, missing the ability to love:
not me, not my sister, not herself.

The family that's left is weakened; its will
to keep on going, its cohesiveness is gone.
Like the waters of the Okavongo Delta that
disperse into the Kalahari to vanish with the
change of season, Eva's family has scattered,
thinned out, spread across the country, and,
unlike the waters of the delta that renew
each year, we cannot seem to find again the
strength and determinations that brought her here.

We are ragged at the edges; our boundaries
spread so widely that we have passed each other
by, do not seem to care and will eventually
run out, deplete, and disappear.
There are no more pilgrims among us.

PAPER DOLLS

Images of beauty, classical features, ageless skin,
perfect bodies, paper dolls like real people printed
on cardboard, are punched free by small hands,
lifted up to wait for Prada-Armani knockoffs,
dresses, suits, cut out with round-tip scissors
so adults can skip the kissing of bloodied fingers.

Legs akimbo, backs slouching, tongues sticking
out between soft lips, children focus, eyes
fixed on dark outlines that must be closely clipped.
Fabric folds stiffen into drawn lines, permit no
alterations to tailored clothes and matching, coordinated
accessories—no hand-me-downs here. Cutting,
fitting, tiny tabs clamped well over paper shoulders,

dressed-up dolls are lined up for the fashion show.
Come see, they're ready to go, and little hands guide
the dolls, bump, bump down the invisible
pathway leading out the door. Paper dolls
ripped from flatland into more dimensions leave
behind them floors covered with slashed papers
laced with empty spaces, the human figures taken.

PENELOPE'S HOUSE

Aunt Penelope can sit for hours
cleaning her dollhouse, adding
furniture, rearranging the rest,
weaving wishes and hopes together
into a fraying fabric of dreams.

I like the tiny piano, a parlor grand
like the one she once played,
Hepplewhite chairs, precise in a line,
a breath away from the wall, dining
room table set for uninvited guests,
a kitchen complete but sterile.

A staircase arches upward to a room
with a canopied bed, swirls of flounces,
ruffles, a duvet cover pink and white
enough to widen the eyes of a little girl.
In a closet, miniscule dresses join
an array of blouses, miniature shoes.

The second bedroom has darker furniture,
a striped throw and matching drapes
that hang down in a severe line.
The open closet holds no clothes.
I sense connection, a family whisper.
Penelope's lover disappeared.

I reach out to touch the perfect
pieces, caress the upholstery,
open a door: her voice freezes
my hand's motion. She grabs
my arm from her wheelchair,
looks at the dark empty bedroom.
She watches, waits for somebody
other than me. I hold my breath.

PILLOWS

The stripes on my pillow don't match
where the seams join the two sides.
Shoddy pillow making is like shoddy love making,
forced, painful.
Push and twist,
stuff and shove,
the parts don't mesh, they don't fit,
same as shoes that feel too tight with heavy socks on.

It's no good going on when that happens.
Much better to think of something else,
different and exhilarating.
Riding on a merry-go-round, for example.
Horses start out distinct individuals.
Avoid the ones that don't go up and down: they're a waste of energy.
The others chase each other as they spin,
but even though they go faster,
they never catch up.
I don't want to be on the last one,
all alone and left behind,
as the others gallop off and disappear outside.

The tigers don't go, they don't even move.
Maybe they're dangerous and can't be trusted,
like some people,
like my lover.
From late afternoon business meetings
he'd come home,
hang up his coat,
talk daily trivia,
eat a quick dinner,
go to bed and turn on his side, his back to me.

I would touch him and his flesh was cold, and stayed cold.
When I outlined my body against his, he'd pull away.
No touch or caress could arouse him, so

I would stop and wipe my wet cheeks on the pillowcase.
Staring, without seeing,
I would finally notice that the stripes don't match.

POSSESSIONS

The narrow rectangular
houses, a short row,
a cordon between
the beach and the
highway, attract
the eyes of motorists
relishing the colors
of lime, salmon, peach,
contrasting pastel
shades augmented
by Mondrian lines
of windows, doors,
sparkling glass
outlined in white.

Across the way,
on the palisades,
wrapped in the dark
plastic that doubles
as bedding and clothing,
a ruddy-faced, grimy man
wearing a close-fitting
woolen cap pulled
tight over ears
to keep out daylight sounds,
shakes his lethargy,
stares
across the highway
at the multicolored
houses.

RAINBOW'S END

I slid under the rainbow,
slipping on wetness, legacy
of sprinklers, faux waterfall
mists.

The perfect arc was broken
into splinters pointing
to either end where
my children hid after
leaving, became replacement
treasures for bereaved
leprechauns.

I traversed a rainbow path,
vermillion dawns,
creamy noon-light,
lilac of late afternoon,
deep blue of night
sparkling with silver,
drilled peep holes
for the gods.

Years of perseverance,
I found my children.
They were not as
I remembered them.

SHELTER

A lifetime ago she watched men,
giants in her eyes, armed with clubs,
knives, penetrate a copse like this one.
Forced to run, she screamed, sought
shelter behind her mother's skirt,
her aunt's broad back, any refuge.

Today, it's her grandson she watches
as he climbs the crazed bark of a tree
over tangled limbs, aiming for the top.

In a ten-year-old's summer,
days run fast, still time enough
to test fragile branches, weigh choices,
step with caution as he watches
his grandma below, chooses
to climb down, only half regretful.
He will ask for a story.

She might tell him the one
about the neighbor boy
who gave her a single, jeweled
earring, "found" among his mother's
treasures. She cherished it, hid
it in her bursting satchel when
she crossed the ocean.
She might sing, in her
off-key monotone, a Chanukah
song about candles or games.

Whatever she might choose to tell or sing,
she would smile, put her arms
around him, rock him close.

SPECIAL DAY

Some of these children can't walk to school,
        tie a shoelace, see the face
                of a parent.

In our comfortable world,
        they make us feel ill at ease; we
                set them aside, to live unseen.

They are with us today,
        on wheels that carry them
                to booths where

they crayon elephants
        with golden curls
                and squirrels with wings,

wear painted butterflies on their foreheads.
        Proud to create pipe-cleaner dolls,
                purple cardboard horns

a plastic necklace just like mom's,
        some ask for help, others push
                my hand away, faces determined

under their painted-on flowers.
        Eyes goggle at the puppet clowns,
                performers who fly across the stage,

ethnic dancers, drummers so loud
        the listeners almost tap in rhythm,
                and the smiles they flash are not painted on.

SPIDER WOMAN[2]

When he arrives, hand slack
in his pocket, he will pull out his key,
unhurried, knowing all
that is behind that door,
no surprises, half a lifetime later.
She gobbled him
whole, thirty/forty years ago,
ingested everything he was—
beliefs, tastes, swallowed
it all, swelled up with
dedication, goodwill, and children,
so became his image, that
he doesn't need to look
to recognize her expression
as his own. The door will
open and entering the narrow
hall, he will smell, before
he sees, the person there,
smell the kitchen aroma
caught in her hair, her hands
wet with veggie-wash
and disinfectant, see the smile
same as all days in all years
that have passed.
He is relaxed,
comforted.
Reliable, continuous
is his own little web.

2   Published in *Oberon Poetry*, 2009 annual issue.

THE CHILD BEHIND THE COUCH

Dust fluffs, mite-ridden strips
ripped off the damask sofa
expose the stuffing
to exploration
from small boy
fingers as he settles
down for the night,
zipped into
his sleeping bag.

Late on an unselected,
unplanned day,
he quits the couch,
moves out
under the space bubble sky,
finds a hillock pillow
waiting to be wept on,
not rising until dawn.

His hope is cautious,
a toe in the water,
a coin retrieved
from the genetic
pool, desperate
for a chance.

WANTING FROGS

Mud-slimed, shady banks edge
dirty water—there they are—
tadpoles, black puff bodies,
comet tails quivering toward
clear shallows. My children's

small hands grab—miss. Pollywogs
are fast darters. Latching onto
an old jar, the boys capture muck,
swaying weeds, and creatures.

Even imprisoned, tadpoles change,
adapt to life as amphibians.
My sons stare, impatient
for metamorphosis, wanting
frogs. Look, a few tadpoles
paddle, tiny feet battle,
a child's hand swirls the jar.

No dramatic changes.
Interest fades.
Demand is made for
frogs right now.

I understand them; they
find it very hard to wait.
They are young
and immature.

SPECIAL OLYMPICS

We named her Alice because we knew
from the start she was different from
children of this world. Allie-Allie is the
name she likes, but today, in competition,
she will go by the number worn on her back.
She sits balanced on the saddle, holding
the pommel. Jodhpured knees grip the
horse's flanks, boots shove into stirrups.

Her coaches positioned her, left her.
"Stay there Allie-Allie, wait for us."
Alice knows her job. Under the riding cap,
her face is set, unsmiling, concentrating.
The reliable horse will carry her around
the course, between the fences, just as it
did at the many practices when we
dropped her off and left her there,
not wanting to stay, not wanting to watch.

"Go for the gold, Allie-Allie." Her
fellow riders cheer her on. I don't
want to join in, the outcome, after all,
is guaranteed. Alice will win. All the
athletes will win before the crowd
of family, friends, and volunteers.

The coaches lead the mounts with care
and stop before the judges' stand.
Alice wins her medal. I am glad
that she can do this, even though
we wished for years that she had
been born someone else's daughter.

Alice is lifted down, still not smiling,
receives the medal, the praise,
and a hug from her coaches.

Her head remains bowed. I go
with others to congratulate her,
to embrace her. She accepts my
hug, but her eyes look over my
shoulder, searching the crowd,
seeking a face that will not be there.

THE MOTHER GAME

Crumpled paper litters the carpet
where their sofa once stood.
Dust devils shudder in the moving air
as their bookcases are dismantled.
Two cartons stand, one with her name,
one with his—each contains one half
of the set of china I gave them;
each will go to a different address.

My fury swells at his father for dying,
at his wife for her stubbornness,
her inability to grasp reality,
her ability to injure him.

As a toddler, he fell hard against a table
and cried through the blood, clinging
to my shoulder on the way to the ER.
Through mumps and measles,
broken bones, and accidental hurts,
I was there to comfort him.

I think he is wounded, again.
I think he is grieving,
but he is an adult male now.

I can only reassure him,
hold his hand
until the lawyers cut them apart
and let him heal.

THE STERLING SILVER TEA SET

My mother told me that someday
it would be mine, the tea set
grandma carried all the way
from Liverpool. Old-fashioned
sterling, curlicued with vines,
grape leaves, and tiny fruit,
it wore a patina of tarnish.

In my mind it was elegant,
a treasure too fine for daily use.
My mother never polished it,
never shared its handling with me.
After her death, I claimed it.

Dented on one side, the tea pot
rocked on four bowed legs.
The creamer had a slender,
slightly twisted lip. Of the sugar
bowl's two handles, one was loose
and bent. How careless of grandma
to let it arrive in such bad shape.

The surface of the serving
tray was marred and scratched.
I tried to polish it and found
that as I rubbed and rubbed
the silver wore away. I saw
exposed base metal, lusterless
and dark, deceptive, like
a secret kept from me.

THE WILL

The cameo, a gift from Aunt Louise, who,
like her niece, was born beneath the sign
of the crab, will be passed on to Angela.

The diamond band, relic of divorce, will go
to Margaret, the oldest, a reminder of her
father. His epitaph should have read:
"He kept no promises but somehow
kept his daughters' love."

The chain of gold links that once encircled
her neck, and now will nearly go around her
waist, goes to Angela who admired it.

Their grandma's sapphire ring, her ruby earrings,
she will leave to Margaret; to Angela, the ring and
bracelet of Florentine gold set with diamond chips.

Her sister, Bella, will inherit, bequeathed for the
second time, their mother's pearls. The lapis
pendant Papa gave her will go to Bella, too.

She will not let them squabble over baubles,
will not let avarice infect their friendship
or weaken family ties. They must
weep for her and not for ornaments.

When they wear these jewels
they will remember her:
the sister who shared a childhood,
and celebrated joyous times,
and mourned when loved ones died;
the vital woman who carried her
daughters across the playground,
comforted them in times of fear and
pain, heard their confessions of doubt,

held their hands through love and losses,
cradled their babies in her arms.

Her list complete, she settles into
the flat world where every inch is hers.
The sheet that wrinkles when the mattress
pad bunches up, forcing her spine against
the ridges. The covers that shift, exposing
her bony toes to the regulated air, stale
sometimes, but precious.

She is bolstered by the slumping
pillows that scrunch down. They need
to be plumped up but every turn's a
strain and her arms are dotted with the
round band-aids that cover needle marks.

Her hands, thin-skinned, but not
yet liver-spotted, hold the satin
jewelry box, protect the pile of
glittery objects spread over the
mound of her legs. Her fingers
touch each piece of jewelry, caress
the smoothness of the metal,
trace the outlines of each gem.
She takes each piece, holds it for
a moment against her cheek,
replaces it inside the box
and shuts the lid.

LOST SIBLING

Somewhere here among the sparse furniture of the Mojave,
we connected from time to time. The spaces between
connections stretched out, became more frequent. Granite
boulders, before they weathered into pebbles, slivered
into flakes, powdered into granules, echoed her whistle.
She used it, by blood right, to command my attendance.

Particles of sand, whipped by grasping dirt-pinching winds,
penetrated my ankles, pitting my skin so that tiny holes appeared.
I seemed to be harboring a colony of insects that would bore
their way through my flesh, eating me from the inside out.
She never noticed. Changes not seen did not exist for her.

Until this year, she waited here for me, took this chance for a
vicarious wallow in my secret life and hated me for living such
a life. She accepted trophies, verifiers of my stories, assuagers
of my guilt. I knew she would never follow me, but I met her and
her nervous, painful laughter as though I thought she could.

Our conversations, circular and plain, a litany of parents, cousins,
progeny and such, questions polite, answers trite, all flew from
our mouths and missed our ears. Words spun out and vanished.
Sentences spread themselves so thin they attenuated into wisps
of air. Photographs faded, the subjects frozen as they were.

Somewhere out there we lost each other. The desert spreads in all
directions. There are snake and lizard trails among the low-growing
wolfberry, the roots of mesquite. Sand drifts into small piles that
deceive me into thinking they are footprints. She might collapse out
here, splay out, desiccate in the air, bleach in the sun, undiscovered.

At some time, if I were to search again, there might appear above her
hiding place a Star of David. No, not that, and certainly there would
not be a cross. Most likely, I would find a single stick, stripped of
bark, unfinished, standing straight up in windblown isolation.

SIBLINGS

My sister ordered out a copy of her birth certificate
and called me when she found anomalies:
three pregnancies when there are only two of us.
There was a stillborn.
What was it? Boy or girl?
What would it have looked like?
Maybe it would have been wrapped
in a blanket of tenderness,
something we never had, my sister and I.

I knew somehow, and, years ago, I asked my mother.
She denied it ever had existed, but she lied; she often did.
She shared nothing of herself.
I never knew her girlhood.
Her memories were dark inside of her,
growing like mushrooms,
never to see the light,
unshared, as was her intimate self.

Duty made her pregnant.
Obligation raised us.
Her small understanding was
bounded on one side by food and clothes
and on the other by rules
written in some inherited code
translated into limits without care or reason.
Nice girls don't touch themselves there,
but I did—and it was scary.
Nice girls don't talk about sex,
which meant she didn't have to.
She didn't have to love me either.
Bad as I was, who would?

My dead sibling would have.
He/she would have held me,
stroked my cheek,

sung me to sleep,
told me stories of wonderful lands
that I would go to someday.
He/she would have cried with me when friends left me out of plans,
forgot me again;
shared my sorrow when a first love turned sour
and left me bleeding.
One dead baby caring for another,
each one resting in an unmarked grave somewhere
memorialized as a blank filled in
on the birth certificates
of two surviving sisters.

WHITE RICE

A necessary culinary corollary in the Philippines,
this need came with her to fabled America:
"Brown rice is no good, breaks the rice cooker."
Sweet potato vines imported into Filipino markets,
along with dried, boney fish, pancit noodles,
are trusted foods. Most local meats, fruits
are suspected, untried, condemned.

Church-going on Sunday, where Tagalog speakers
mingle, she refuses, awaits neighbors to knock
on her door as they always did, trudging through
dirt alleys to vent troubles, gossip about husbands,
kids, slowly, slowly, for there was always time.
Rush, bustle, fear of hurtling traffic, terror of driving
stymies her reaching out to co-expatriates.

A small internet café, patronized by locals, was hers
until outliers came from beyond the pineapple
plantation, forced her evacuation, confiscation
of her livelihood—homelessness. Internet, accessible
for complaints to family back home, led, in her search
for companionship, to a chat with an unknown man.
An invitation to the house horrified her daughter.

Dusting, vacuuming, washing, sewing for her grandson;
helping with his preschool workbook, all homey chores,
but outside, work for strangers—scary, to be resisted.
Depressed, resentful, sleepless at night, napping
during the day, her self-inflicted isolation not clearly
understood, she finds new aches and pains every day.
"I was never sick at home. Didn't need insurance."

Here, now, this future with white rice three times a day,
even with the Filipino foods, is less a comfort
than a reminder of her lost homeland.

WIDOW TO WIDOW

Barefoot, she enters uninvited. In this
Filipino village people flow like a river
from one front door to the next.

Finding she is three years my senior,
she grimaces, bares crooked stained teeth
so close together they overlap.

Only three? I peer at her dark face,
cross-hatched with spidery lines,
sprinkled with sparse, grey chin hairs.

In garbled English she wants to talk
widow to widow, as though a common
bond of mutual loss transcends culture,

time, place. Maybe—but our histories
are not shared, our backgrounds,
lifestyles so disparate.

She wanders into neighbors' homes at will.
I need an invitation to invade a private space.
Everyone in this village is her extended family.
In my city, people retreat behind good fences.
Her eyes see my world in television, her ears
hear travelers' tales.
I have just been introduced to hers.

Tagalog, the local Visayan dialect, limits
Conversation; questions, answers interrupted
by visitors, in-laws I have just met.

My grandson's new-found grandpa, gleeful,
parades him up and down the street,
in and out of small sari-sari stores,

admired for his fair complexion.
He is here by inheritance, blood
ties to his mother's family.

I am an honored guest, also a curiosity,
an exotic in this rural town. I swelter
in the damp heat. Someone turns

on an electric fan. Added to the clamor
of voices, the widow and I cannot
hear each other. We give up.

Widowly feelings, sentiments,
stories common to both of us
will have to be left to imagination.

AS A CHILD

I ran after her,
chased her, crying,
"Wait for me, wait for me."
She walked on, turned.
It was not my mother.

TEENAGER

I ran away from her,
confided in my friends,
told my diary,
rejected every gift
she tried to give me.

ADULT

Releasing her from state hospital,
where I had to commit her,
a psychiatrist told me
she was an incomplete personality,
unable to love, not even herself.

UNCAGED

Like ornaments spaced
to show off glorious
colors, a small flock,
birds of unlike feathers,
flashed. Five little handfuls
of purple, crimson, emerald

iridescence, improbable
in this climate zone, tropically
derived, imagined to be
hiding in dense green wetness.
Here, restless, unable to be still,
they scattered like fireworks.

My grandson,
had he shared this fabulous
scene, would choose to
chase, corner the fleeing birds.
For toddlers—and not only toddlers—

possession is the true reality
until they may come to understand
all things rare and beautiful, even love,
can be treasured,
                never caged.

WALKING AT SUNRISE

It is moon-dead outside. In the remains of the night,
I imagine the wind sucked into spectral lungs, exhaled
enough to float the first birds of dawn. Grey-soft
feathers whisper past me; the olive green of a night
heron's back shows color as light parts pre-dawn black.

White under-wings flash, a perched junco swells
its throat, warbles into the silence, mimicked
by a mockingbird as it trills the threads
of dawn into the orange webbing of morning light.

Time past on extraordinary days, we woke at four a.m.,
raced to reach a canyon of red rocks, see the sun rise
over rosy jagged hills, pristine, enchanted.

Ordinary days were a flurry of kids,
lunches, cheek-pecked kisses.
Any leftover dawn ate itself up,
left me no time to sigh or admire
the fading beauty.

When they moved away,
one by one, it was at midday,
with no slow unfolding,
no lingering mystery.

WHY?

A grey veil, wind-woven, curtains the sun.
He squints through wet lashes, frowns
at his bearing tree, watches its wind-sleeved
limbs smack the trunk, limb crotch
                    shaking.

These branches will not support his weight.
Years ago, when his smaller self proved
a burden, they rocked him, rocked
his cradle, both to the ground,
                    falling.

He stands on the same ground
deep in the slough of not
understanding, racked
by too much, or not enough,
                    frantic.

There! A building, a beam,
high, sturdy, waiting. The rope
cast over it will drape his shoulders
in rough comfort, release him
                    kicking.

A snap,
a flash of memory,
he forgot
                    to tell them why.

THE IMPORTANT THINGS

In a ten-year-old's summer, days run fast,
always too short; still time enough to test
the fragile branch in a treetop, weigh
choices, to step or not; time enough
for his bubba standing below to call
up a warning to take care.

A lifetime ago, she watched grown men,
glints in her eyes, armed with clubs
and knives, penetrate a copse like this one.
Forced to run for home, she yelled a warning
of pogrom, as she ran to hide behind
her mother's skirt, her aunt's apron,
sought any refuge, any open door. Escape!

Today, she had only one charge—to watch
her grandson's slender body descend
from the tree, heave a sigh of relief
when, safe beside her, he would ask
for another story about old Latvia.
She would relate her memories
of family and friends; the old rabbi
who came with them to Boston,
Hanukkah parties with gelt and dreidels,
candles in the synagogues, dancing
at her cousin's wedding. She wanted
him to hear only the important things.

NEW GENERATION

His six-foot-four frame bends
way over to hug me. I think
back to days when I could carry him
or an earlier time when my phone
rang at 4 a.m., an infant's wailing
breaking into my dawn, and I heard
"Well, here he is, your grandson."

Over bagels and lox we recall when
I took him to Roswell, place of aliens,
where we studied rockets, shot one
off, competed to send his higher.
We visited White Sands, stopped
off at Carlsbad to ogle nature's power.
Today, he tells me more about

his work. Highly specialized, its
place is the "cloud," the electronic
trope around which I feel hugely
ignorant, barely comprehending
the technology, but finding
the start-up ventures

fascinating. This is his first
visit to me on his own, and
he promises he will come
again, and that sounds very good.
He will bring with him his
now live-in girlfriend.

WIND DANCE

Waves toss the air-filled
plastic ball, or breezes send it
bouncing down the wrong path.
A child with quivering lips
and damp disappointment
runs after it as it rolls away
with its bright clown colors.

Too light to make a hollow
in the sand, followed by the child
with a hand too small
to gain a hold, arms
too short to grasp the whole,
the beach ball, squeezed
hard, is propelled away,
as loved things are when
held too tight. A toddler

finds the ball too wide,
but as little arms lengthen,
so pleasure wanes. Beach
balls are for innocents
to lose, grown-ups to chase,
retrievers of a wayward toy,
consolers for loss.

TIDE TABLES

Measured at the harbor's mouth, ocean
tides rise, fall, graph as smooth curves.
Tiny alterations mingle, homogenize
as in a visage glimpsed after absence,
so you can say to me "You look
the same after all this time."

To scan a face briefly
is to miss miniscule
changes, less resilient cells,
a hair of different color,
a wrinkle trickling along
the mouthward path.

No sea change, but one age
sliding into another.

If the ocean were de Leon's mythic fountain,
elders could submerge, ebb with low tide,
emerge a youth on a creeping wave;
follow again a singular life,
the awkward, uncoordinated child,
the child labeled smart
when beautiful was wanted,
chosen last for the team,
wearing hand-me-downs.
I had a hard time saying thank you.

College, a degree in compromise.
Singlehood—work, play, sex.
Marriage a safe haven,
an adjustment that never jelled,
still produced children.
A constant challenge,
they were the face of time,
calendar of undeniable mortality
moving at an accelerated pace.

Like a lot of kelp fronds, swaying
in opposite directions, they were
stubborn—pliable,
eager—resistant,
suggestible possibly,
restless to be away—

I begin to see
what once was pioneer becomes
the ordinary; the tides of culture,
waves of morality change,
I pretend not to notice swelling surges,
the pulling of the currents,
the ocean's grainy floor
becoming more visible.

I keep on swimming.

III
Daily Life at Home
Crossroads of the World

DANCES AT WEDDINGS

Old wives say the spasmodic
jerk of limbs, symptom of the
tarantula's bite, adapted into
an Italian folk dance. Arms
fling wide, knees kick legs out,
as though struck by a doctor's
rubber-headed hammer. All yell
"Buona fortuna, buona fortuna."

In the hora, in a circle, in a
grapevine step, bodies bob up
and down to the hypnotic beat
of a Klezmer band. The bride
and groom are hoisted, seated
in chairs, raised high by friends,
paraded around to the shouts
of "Mazel tov, mazel tov."

In the tarantella, in the hora, feet plunge
up and down, hips twist, hands grapple,
frantic for a hold, elbows link, shoulders
are gripped. Dancers swing each other
faster and faster to the rhythmic drums,
blaring horns, snapping fingers. Holding
hands, the lines of celebrants circle in
caracole fashion toward the center to
surround the newly married couple.

Encircled, stands the farmer
who has chosen his wife.

Encircled, stands the wife who
will someday choose the child.

The child will choose the dog.
The dog will choose the cat.

The cat will choose the mouse.
The mouse will not choose.

The cheese will stand alone.

In the playground, where all
the children dance around to
be selected one by one, there
is one not chosen, one left out,
one standing isolated, fearful,
hoping someday for a chance
to be included inside the circle.

IS IT FUN YET?

Picture a Caucasian couple, heterosexual with
undyed hair, unwrinkled skin, denture-less smiles.
Their eyes have no blue pouches, need only reading
glasses, need no hats to shade sun-loving skin.
He wears a pastel polo shirt, polyester pants,
and saddle shoes. She wears a flowered dress of
mid-calf length and shoes with heel straps and open toes.

Home is a beige condominium with vinyl-tiled
floors in kitchen and in bathroom; nylon carpet
(stain resistant) for the combination living-dining
space; twin beds, two wicker nightstands, high
windows, draped and usually locked.
There are two television sets for nights
the other couples can't come in for bridge,
or days his golf game is rained out or
her exercise-for-fitness class is cancelled.
One wall and a tabletop display varied sizes of
framed photographs of children, children's children,
brother, sister, other outside folks.
She touches them with a long-distance finger
then wipes the fingerprints away with care.

They folded up their lives, cast off the old
cocoon of neighborhood, gave up their rights
to make some choices, settled into
this marshmallow world where filtered air
smells sweet and handymen fix broken things,
responding to a telephoned request.
Silence is not shattered here by screaming
kids or barking dogs or screeching brakes;
the street has traffic bumps.
The faces at the poolside lounge are homogeneous,
the proper color, deepened only by a suntan tinge.
The singles population seems to increase steadily
from new arrivals or from those who lost their partners

while already here. Wisely, they have separated into
self-contained, and largely female, groups.

Sometimes, when the couple watches television
news they see the homeless sprawling
on the sidewalks, prey to stalkers; witness
parents weeping for their children shot amid
the infestation spread by inner city gangs;
gape at third-world tribes that murder
thousands, even newborns, in continual vendettas
washed by blood from mutilated limbs; see news
anchors with their regulation faces, even-voiced,
narrating clips of bombed-out buildings of the
new, proliferating Sarajevo slums, of bodies strewn
across the earth, distended bellies caused by
plague, starvation, dehydration, or whatever
sickening affliction ails them now.

Since they lost interest in the comics, newspapers
are irrelevant and usually too liberal to trust;
television gives them all they need to know of
politics and, in addition, shows them current
local interest items such as earthquake damage,
car hijackings, and an unplanned, riveting police
chase of a fleeing suspect, filmed from helicopters
and a freeway overpass.

On occasion a slight tremor of the ground, or
shattering storm of wind and rain reminds
them of the natural limits to mortality,
but otherwise they fear no riots, smell no
fires, dodge no bullets, have no case of AIDS
in their community. The outside world slides
off their backs with pieces of it landing
in the toilet to be flushed away.

They pay homage to idyllic cutouts,
representing Nancy-Ronny dreams.
They honor this, the theme park way of life.
But please remember! It's not Never Never

Land, for Peter Pan is unreliable and not
allowed. He only wants to play, untouched
and ageless. He asks a solitary question,
the only one that interests him at all:

IS IT FUN YET?

COUNTRY CLUB

From her lounge she watches
faceless boys in tennis shorts
pick up soggy towels, rush
to the terrace to gather glasses
drained of daiquiris.

Beyond the flagstone patio,
a man in beige,
with one hand gloved, tees off.

Anxious for her tennis partner,
she endures the ennui
of another silky afternoon.
Couples she knows sit nearby,
don't ask her to join them.

A message comes. She
leaves. Her partner's
husband claimed priority.

Her house, high-ceilinged,
has many rooms. They echo
to the sound of the turning key.
She sees the fading light
lap up the orange sun.

Soon, the dark of the moon steals
the purple from the cosmos, leaves
them ash-white in the star light.

Night breezes wrap cloud around
cloud into a mysterious shape
that makes a dent like a head
in the pillow next to hers.

BEAD SELLER

I enter a narrow shop beside
the boardwalk at Venice Beach.
The seller in a tie-dye dress hangs
long strings of beads, brown-faux
amber, purple-glass amethyst.

Bead curtains divide the shop
into even smaller cubicles, dark
beyond the reach of sunbeams,
smelling of mold and urine, floored
with sand ground into linoleum
remnants or pocked cement.

A skinny, young girl sidles out
from behind the counter,
grabs for a half cookie
someone discarded on the floor,
sees me watching, gobbles it.

The sun begins to set,
cheating her of warmth
as she wanders outside.
Flesh puckered from the chill,
her legs are wound around
with a stringy terry cloth.

She reaches out a hand, palm
upward, beseeching the tourists,
who came to gape at eccentric locals,
to comfort her with the affection
of silver.

FISHERMEN ON THE ROCKS

Rod tips edged with green, light-reflecting
strips angle up and out, surround
the fishermen with a magic circle.
Now I see a dozen men,
strung out around the point,
cast base metal weights into darkness,
guided by intuition tinged with faith.

A glowing rod tip bends
with a sudden tug that cold hands
can't feel through the bottom-dragging surf.
This may be the big one.

A ray, dredged up from the bottom,
lies flapping in a flashlight aura,
its soft, ivory belly exposed,
its gills vibrating,
until someone retrieves the hook
and the ray flaps into the water,
tail butchered off, now also defenseless.

A teenager waves the tail
overhead, threatening neighbors
with the stinger. The tongues
of his shoes hang out; he teeters.
Madre, sitting, yells at him,
yells at two little ones
chasing each other on the flat
asphalt behind the wire rail.

Families clamber all over the
forbidden rocks, fishing
until moonrise, or the fog rolls in,
or the beach patrol comes.

REFLECTIONS IN A WINDOW

After sundown, from inside a brightly lit café,
I gaze at the bar across the street, the homeless man
peering in the window. I see reflected in the glass
eyes of people behind me staring at the back
of my head. Mouths open, close like fish underwater,
soundless with hinged jaws. Someone's face
has features that hover on the edge of familiarity.

Chandelier reflections waver, their lights like candles,
flames shivered by breezes, in the wake of passersby.
Vague forms of waiters move between tables,
turn solid as they move past, morph again into ethereal.

Conversation, laughter, mask the disappearance
of the real people. Glass aliens have taken over
minds and bodies, made them transparent,
become their cold custodians.

More enter the café, melt into the common
room behind me as I focus on the bar
across the street, the homeless man
peering in—both solid, clear, and real.

OUTRAGE

Hall empty, dark as usual.
I opened the door,
WOW—
chaos, piles of clothes,
books, pictures, drawers emptied.
In panic I screamed, again screamed
until a neighbor ran up, checked
for intruders. GONE.

Police—no forced entry,
lock picked?
Fingerprints fruitless,
left black powder
on tan carpet.
Security guard—where
were you when my gold was taken?
No recall of all the pieces,
just memories of buying abroad
when we first saw Paris, Rome.

Jewelry worth a lot but
not as much as my tranquility,
safety inside my castle.

Tim from downstairs brought
turkey soup, helped me.
I stayed, toughed it out,
chose to face sleeplessness,
planned to do what?
Called my sons, said "Don't
come, I'm okay, well, not okay,
unharmed, well, not unharmed,
but not bruised or knocked out
or shot."

Sleep fitful, stunned beyond
comprehension.
Dawn. With light came
exhaustion, desolation,
facing clean-up.

Neighbors
cleared a path,
all concern, confusion,

noiseless, they said,
heard nothing, saw less.

Bodies in action,
drawers, shelves,
closets restocked,
BUT I am shaken,
lock the door with my new key
just to go downstairs.

Intruders—I saw low-browed
hulks mindlessly homing
in on cash, gold, heedless
of my privacy, vulnerability,
rapers of my intimate corners,
special places. They stole
my peace of mind,
leaving me with an imperative,
a struggle, a fight
to get it back.

FRUSTRATION

Full of red sugar water,
a tube bottomed with
plastic flowers hangs,
sausage-like, waiting
for barely visible, fast-
beating wings, iridescent
green, purple-tinged feathers,
an arced beak, slender
tongue probing into
miniscule openings.

Not even cooed at,
mocked, or pecked at,
the cylinder hangs
around—a feeding
failure. I let it stay
until sugar crystals
scab the interior,
then pack it into a carton
with objects I have tired
of or given up on, throw
the lot into the trash,
ineligible for recycling.

ROMANCE

Around the water fountain, precious
ollas leaned against the stucco wall,
women talk of men who treated them
with care and held them safe.

Before the unlit fire, nutmeats in a
basket, shells strewn on the ground,
the women laugh about their men, their vanity,
their foolish pride, their weaknesses.

Beside the chopping block, mincing
onions, slicing mushrooms, grating cheese,
the women list their lovers' presents,
counting trivialities as mattering.

One will leave the fountain, shivering
the shawl over her shoulders and head.
One will turn her back on the firepit
and walk, head bowed, into the forest.
One will leave the kitchen, the house
to walk outside seeking solitude.

Each will conjure up a lover lost,
a vanished mate, a
partner never known and
wonder why she feels
diminished, smaller, valued
less than when she stood
with others, telling lies.

"APRIL IS THE CRUELEST MONTH"

thanks to TSE

First:

Paper clippings strewn across my desk like ragged, white rose petals.
Each bear an all-important note. Grist for the mill of IRS.

One, a bill for very expensive shoes. The only ones not painful
on my heavily doctored feet. Clearly a medical expense.

Another, a charge for a gourmet meal at Michael's in Santa Monica,
the remains of the meal in their Styrofoam container handed out
with a smile to a homeless woman, obviously a charitable gift.

A list of books of poetry from various readings and venues.
Necessary to keep up with the local scene, of which I am
a participant: this must be education expense.

Gasoline, automobile wear and tear driving to my artist friend
with whom I have published a book, planning to make lots of money.
Must be a business expense.

Second:

Local politicians exhort,
schools, libraries they support,
we cannot let them come up short.
Property taxes we cannot abort.
Half are due in April.

April tears and April rains wash money and soil away.
We hope to see both kinds of green and rainbow blooms in May.

REINCARNATION

Ocean breezes puff out a red, green,
yellow striped tent like a jib sail.
Shadows from fly-over gulls
skim across the drooping canvas.
A guitar player, hair skinned back
into a pony knot, chants *hari, hari,*
open your hearts to Krishna,
in Sanskrit without translation.

Odors of rice, curry, saffron mingle
with the sweaty odor of men
in billowy trousers, women
in saris, infants lightly swathed,
red-faced from the heat. Girls glitter
with silver, fan their fingers
backwards, hop to drum beats.
Their ankle bells clatter.

Some here worship Krishna, pray
for rebirth, a better life. Nonbelievers
revel in the warmth of welcome
and a summer Sunday festival.
Heat, drums, chants blend for me
into my private vision of Krishna,
dark enigma, flute player.

Through my haze, I see two young men
pass through the tent, before the dais.
Careful with their surfboards, they
don't look around, don't pause. I watch
their single-minded march, wonder
if an unknown god has granted them
reincarnation as worshippers of surf.

VENICE PIER

Shore lights reflect on water
wrinkled by little waves
that *shoosh* as they hit the pilings.

A mound of shucked mussels
lies next to a trash can
that stinks of rotting squid.

"No overhead casting,"
but walkers duck flying bait
and lead weights hurled into darkness.

Rods stuck in rail holes, taut lines
are watched obliquely by men,
knives held in calloused hands.

A pregnant woman pushes a stroller.
Two preteen boys circle around
the end platform on in-line skates.

A blond woman with stringy hair,
wearing a worn sweatshirt, stands
next to a bag of rags and fish guts.

Three Japanese girls, still wearing
hats, sit on a neat, folded blanket
watching a male friend tend his line.

Alla, asoko, over there, a variety
of yells as many hurry, push to see
the catch of an unexpected lobster.

Each rail section harbors its own group.
I watch from an unclaimed spot,
amazed at how intense the action is.

The homeless man, sober just now,
floats from one place to the next
giving advice.

CITY DWELLER

I don't know true silence.
Even in the early-a.m.-tossing-in-the-bed time,
I sense a muffled hum
as city-bred ants
tunnel through midnight depths,
where, despite their hush,
they release noises.

Tire treads squish on wine-dark asphalt.
A helicopter rotor thrums,
spying on a vagrant who can't sleep.
A siren clamors.
It's over on the boulevard
where night people wait,
hear neon gas buzz through tubing.

I breathe easy at engine turnover,
door slam, dog bark. I freeze
at the unnameable. No one's
here to still my alarm,
shelter me from a face
half-remembered,
fuzzy features twisted,
mouthing
a name just over the horizon.

TOWN AND COUNTRY

The red-crested woodpecker snaps back
its head, releases its powerful beak,
and hammers into the bark of a
truncated tree limb, seeking grubs.
The bird's rat-a-tat rhythm counterpoints
the rattle of a snake's tail as it
slithers into a rat's nest.
The rodents panic, forget the
Pied Piper and swarm into town.
They swim through sewers, claw
up cement slopes, and hide
from daylight in the alleys.
They abandon the sidewalk
trails that wind between the
high-rise groves of marble walls,
to the workers' swarm that commutes
every day to the hive of the city,
dependent on its sweet rewards.

Inside the multi-levelled structures,
the staff inhabit their cells to watch
their outboxes grow and tend their faxes.
Their bosses seat themselves in the
boardroom around the ovoid table,
under the baleful glare of the portrait
of the company's founder. Their lawyers
and their bankers feed them lunch and
mergers and watch them swallow both as
they belch out decisions that alter
other people's lives. Enriching or
destroying, the deals are closed.

Window glass reflects the walls of
the neighboring buildings as shaky
outlines in pane-trimmed rectangles
that hold the red glare of sunset,

the blinding brilliance of the dying sun.

Elevator doors spew out the members
of the day tribe: the hacks, the clones,
the professionals, the managers, the CEOs.
Some descend into the underground to
be shuttled away in crowded cylinders.
Others, strapped into vehicles, enclosed
by locked steel doors, flee back to their

country homes before the night
residents make the scene.

The rats return at night; so do the
children suckled on muscatel.
The dealers, traffickers, users come;
their pricked flesh puckers to kiss
the blessed needle, to drink peace
until they rock upon the sidewalk flats.
They bow to the darkness, to the
slow rhythms of insistent drums that
beat inside their heads. They bang
their foreheads against block walls,
hammer them against curbs until
they bleed. Then, when their hair is
crusted red with blood, they can
sink into oblivion for the night.

MORNING WITH RADIO

I roll out of bed into the gray light of morning,
clench my toes over the tight weave of carpet,
also gray, record in my journal my dream,
stumble toward reality into the kitchen,
fill the grinder with special roasts, mountain-
grown in Kenya, Costa Rica, Ethiopia.

Radio news, my chance to jump clear
of dreams, fill my ears with messages
of false hope for serious world change.
I twist the dial to find some low-key
cheerfulness, avoid duplicating
another painful, ordinary morning.

I dawdle over breakfast, study a newspaper
photo of an old woman pulled out alive
from earthquake rubble in Iran, a miracle.
Radio reporters echo the columns
on political appointments, corruption,
high profile trials. I stick to my coffee,

my reading. Delay the emotions that
surface when I write, the compulsions
that drive me to the phone to plan every
hour of approaching days. Radio voices,
my sole companions, fresh coffee, folded
paper, tricks to ease into a livable day.

CONSTRUCTION ZONE

Rectangles, rhombi, trapezoids
crafted by carpenters,
no time to round corners.
Boards nailed, stapled, slap-dash,
splinters, sawdust plopped out
like horse droppings.

Power saw *buzz*, drill *whirr* follows
me through the swish
of my shower into the morning paper.
Circus of noise tents my mind,
ideas circle around, around,
scared to stop, afraid the racket

will dim their brilliance.
A sudden disappearance
at four-thirty p.m., plywood strips,
plank tips, connectors, bent nails
swept into dust pans, tossed—
men, hardhats, tool belts, boots
stashed inside a Trojan Horse

built today so they can all lurk
inside waiting to pounce while
I dream of smooth finishes,
textured walls, varnished doors.
The night wears away
in dark, sweet silence until—

7:30 a.m. They erupt out of
a Trojan Horse and bang, clang
hammers, drills, saws, pound;
my dream-memories
smashed, my dawdle
into pleasant day destroyed.

FOUR-OH-FIVE

With unevenness in the motion,
some cars pull forward, some,
in Doppler dizziness, seem to slide back,
string toys tugged by a giant
amused as vehicles struggle
to push into any slight space.
Solitary drivers pinned behind
steering wheels drum on the dash,
metronomic to rhythms
that circulate between rolled-up
windows—classical, jazz, rock, rap,
a pastiche of crazed radio patter,
a quilt of sound over bleating horns.

A sporty two-seater, one red fender
buckled, staunch in its lane possession,
surrenders, reluctant to advances
from a pick-up with a chassis
levered way above normal height.
A rocking van stuffed with bouncing
teenagers drives toward its finish
line, south of the airport, home turf.

Now the truth of time tweaks
the thrust of urgency.
The failure of punctuality
dares my brain to seek a new
excuse—traffic is such a cliché,
but the reflected sun glares
off a rear window blind me,
distract me from my focus
on my required destination,
my expected explanation.

BEYOND THE DOOR

Tall, wide, its gray front face gouged
and scarred, the door's square window,
reinforced with wire mesh, opens
to the schoolroom scene beyond.

A well-nourished student wearing
a school sweatshirt, cargo pants,
watches the desk hoppers, seeks
a friend to sit with in the back,
away from teacher's eagle eyes,
ready, after swift comparison,
to edit his homework.

Another one in trousers too short,
a shirt too large, eyes the
students' backpacks, harborers
of the lunch he lacks.
He too heads for the back
of the room, where he can
close his ears, dream up excuses
for a week of absences.

SECURITY ALERT

Visibility is low; the flashing signal
and the foghorn are not working.
A boater churns his paddles, thrusts
his red kayak toward the breakwater.

Fog skirts the water, hovers above
the wavelets, lets the kayak insert
its pointed bow into the space.

A rasping bark carries over the water,
augmented by fog, louder than expected.
Two round, black lumps rise, hunker down
with the wave action—sea lion heads.

The barking sound repeats; the two
black lumps reverse, head for the end
of the rocks. Their mother has called
them back and, like all well-trained
babies, they change course.

The kayak starts to follow, falters
as they beat him around the point.
The channel is socked in, and he must
hurry back. Even if the warnings start,
he cannot see or, probably, be seen.

Sea lion mother does her own
security alert, but she knows
exactly what the danger
is and where it's at.

COMMUNICATION

A share of nothing equals nothing.
Zero does not evolve.
It stays open like the searching
mouth of an infant, sucking
everything: a breast, a finger,
a neck (as when I held my baby,
head bobbling, against
my shoulder).

Promises were hidden everywhere.
All that was needed was to suck
them out and in, or hold them with
the tight fist of babyhood and lie,
full tummy round, legs drawn and
kicking against the uncovered air.

Promises were squeezed hard
and oozed into shapeless days,
long bouts of silence. Years,
left unattended, sailed like
derelict boats around cipher
islands, circling, unable to
stage a fruitful landing.

Zeroes have a use, a function,
a value, a place.
Harness them.
Speak through them.
Listen for an echo,
a question, a response,
an understanding.

A PAIRING (November 1, 1999)

Two mourning doves are outlined,
framed in a space defined by their
pairing, one at each end of a branch.

Separated, chirpless, not sharing twitters
or tender beak stabs, their feathered
chests puffed out, a show for unseen
others, they look past each other. Beady
eyes avoid come-hither glances.

Love sublimates into seed-searching,
desire into picking of nits from the
down under their own wings,
longing into sharpening of beaks on
the branch, close to another food source
found on underleaf and bark slough.

Focused on a new and selfish need,
they fly apart with goodbye
waves of wings.

THE SHOWER

We, all women, sit in soft, upholstered
chairs. We watch each other and the
gifts we brought wrapped in pink, or
blue, or yellow paper, covered with
smirking teddy bears or baby rattles.

The guest of honor, bulky in her flowered
dress, shakes her belly when she laughs,
even though her face is flushed and
she is short of breath. She quips about
weight gain and swollen ankles. Most
of us nod our heads with understanding,
our mouths are busy with sips of
wine, bits of cheese or reminiscences.

She lifts a present, opens and admires
it, then passes it around. Inside she
feels a sudden stabbing thrust.
She picks another gift and reads the
card aloud while all applaud. Again
she feels a rolling pull, a twinge,
a surge, a pinching tweak of pain.

Each opened ritual gift is followed
by an inner kick, a turn, a shift inside
her womb, a punch, a shove from
rib cage to cervix. He lets her know
that he is there, the unseen guest
who lolls in his lullaby cradle,
rocked by amniotic waves.

Feel the bumps his limbs make,
high up, close to your heart.
Pay attention while you can,
while you are still connected.
He will not be there long.
He will not be there long enough.

STILLNESS MATTERS

When the temblor is over
and rocks from the
neighboring hillside
stop crashing down,

when a man and woman no
longer yell invectives at each
other so the hidden little ones
can uncover their ears,

when a siren ceases its
wail after forcing through
traffic in a panic to reach
the hospital in time,

when the roomful of
people stop jabbering
with words as empty
as Swiss cheese holes,

when silence has
devoured all it can,

stillness is left.
Stillness matters.

A YEAR FROM NOW

Hang the rhetorical, feathery, pine-needled boughs.
Circle the lion-head knocker with holly, a red-berried wreath.
Garnish the limbs of front-lawn trees with black wire vines,
marked off by saffron, vermillion, or lilac electric light bulbs.

The little spruce is pagan.
It swells with delicate galls,
with swarms of globes
that mirror the silver drool
of tinsel in their crimson
surfaces, fragile and smooth.

Below cower the cardboard bones,
remains of cartons, cosseted by tissue
paper shreds. Once they sheltered
video games, or furry creatures,
computerized, advertised, plucked
from well-stocked shelves of
clones and imitations. Once they
hid the prizes from premature,
presumptuous, small, persistent
fingers. Now they are free to
scatter their innards over the floor.

In a few days, all of this will segue
into the following sequence:
        We will start the countdown.
        We will do it all again
        a year from now.

IV
Ghosts in the Mist
The World of Nature

THE BIRDS & THE BEES
& THE FLOWERS

In a thin curve, the beak penetrates
the stamen orifice. The long tongue
sucks flower excretions, nectar
the bird swallows many times a day
to fill its tiny stomach, the wings so fast
they border on invisible, burn energy.

Receiving the thrust of the bird,
the stationary flower plays its role,
exposing purples, oranges,
to attract, to tease, to accept
bird-brought gifts into its fickle
heart. Blooms open out and up.
Paradise comes to the flower.

Bees push their way
between heart and lip
of the pollen source, zigzag home,
engorge the cells,
perfect hexagons, sculptures
in wax, with food for the
queen's table, bassinets

for her babies, honey
for the universe. Triad of life
continuing so long as
Hummingbird, the great warrior
of the Pueblo people, protects
the symbiotic trio from destruction.

HUNTRESS

In late afternoon, the guide's walkie-talkie sputtered, a number of
lionesses spotted stalking a kill. Off we went to find them, and
in five or ten minutes we did. They were spread out, apparently
watching a clump of bushes that hid an animal. We couldn't see
what it was. We parked, armed with binocs and cameras.

The tracker had been sitting in a seat that projected ahead of the
driver. He climbed back into the open vehicle, the same one we
always used, with no roof and no doors. The guide told us to be
quiet and to sit still and not stand up.

It was getting darker when a lioness moved next to the truck, near
the rear where I was sitting. She had moved up so slowly and
smoothly, I didn't realize she was there, until I turned my head.
She stopped and started a few times, never taking her eyes off
the quarry's probable location, far ahead. She was only a few feet
away from me. No one else was watching her. I remembered that,
in this camp, none of the guides carried a gun.

My god, I thought, how can she tell that I'm not an impala? She
must smell me. I froze and ducked my head, trying to be smaller.
The black gnats were biting something awful, the spray they had
given us didn't work. I was afraid to wave my arms to get rid of
them.

My heart began to pound. I was terrified. Here I was with strangers.
I had to rely on them, and only them, to take care of me. How
did I know I could trust them? How did I know they didn't hate
me? The French who ran the camps in Botswana weren't known
for their generosity to the natives. For all I knew, these men
lumped all non-Africans as the same: selfish, uncaring, seeking
pleasure at their expense. I wasn't like that, but to them I was just
another tourist.

No one in that truck, not my fellow travelers, not the natives,
cared about me. No one there put an arm around me to comfort

me, although they did hold each other, needing the touch of a companion, the reassurance of a friend, the presence of a husband or wife. There probably wasn't any real danger, but still . . .

The lioness moved on. So did all the rest of the pride. Since it was quite dark, the driver started up and we headed back for the camp.

People were griping they couldn't use their cameras, bitching about the gnats, complaining they were desperate for a bath, planning dinner, to meet for dinner.

I wondered if the hunted animal had escaped.

AFTER OCTOBER

Hours seem compressed, days
smaller, more timid. I think of rabbits
blinking at the sun before
they're forced to dive back
into burrows, fearful,
unprepared for crepuscular dimness.

I protest four p.m. twilight,
not ready for street lights
timed to follow the setting sun.
Somewhere underground,
connections, unmanned,
stamp *finis* on the day.

Ocean winds start earlier now,
sneak across empty beaches,
drift the top grains of sand into
stretch marks over beige skin.
My stucco walls are chilled.
My cold hands cheated
of stored-up warmth.

Clocks are treacherous. I'm not
ready for dinner, for hibernation,
for an end to unexpected
happenings, for excitement
ended too soon, for warmth
and heat extinguished.

ASPEN GROVE

Heedless, joyous, kissing
with a liquid rush of love, one
couple carved a pair of initials
in a heart on the virgin bark of a green
aspen, notice to a blasé world of a new,
lasting pairing. Dated it.

Many aspens in this grove witnessed
this burgeoning feeling.
If they did not fall to nature's wrath
or man's cupidity, they would grow
taller than humans, with thickening
bark. The heart stayed almost

whole, splaying out
as the bearing tree widened. Initials
moved apart, defaced or peeled,
twisted askew, rising higher,
higher above the ground. The lovers
themselves grew apart from each

other, cried, as scarred as their carving,
bled inside, did not heal.
The grove lives on, carries remnants
of promises. Parents, children,
grandchildren, none ever search
for the aspen grove, the special tree.
Hikers see, mock the initials,
the bruising of the aspen grove.

AVALANCHE

A blinding whiteness concealing
all faults from view, this bland,
beautiful accessory to danger
hides caverns, sink holes,
skeletons of hapless cows,
even an unfortunate skier,
like the one who struck out,
alone as usual, to break
a virgin path, cut below
Crystal Crag, over buried fences,
above the summer meadow.

Mountain volunteers, sent
to relieve pressure on unstable
slopes, fired a volley,
blasting loose the snow,
burying the single skier
seen too late.

Desperate, they tore at
still cascading snow,
her location imprecise.
In guilt-pained voices
they shouted her name.
More horrified rescuers
clambered over, yelling
as they came—no one
should go out alone—
always take someone
with you—always.

I heard and thought that then
she might never have been
able to travel any distance at all
from her isolated cabin.

BELIEFS

A light beam, arrowed,
pierces a prism and splits,
passes through newborn red,
burgeons toward the
fresh green/wet blue
of a virtual earth,
fades into violet,
penultimate color.

Tetrahedra crystals,
fitted into corners,
severe in isolation,
taut-ridged, allow no room
for chipped edges or
deviations from straight lines.

Irregularities in floors
are met by pedestals
that check imbalances.
Polyhedra hitting the walls
must make them crack or melt
just to preserve their shapes.

The penetrating beam
continues on,
recovers through the cyan
and magenta passages,
channels through the yellow
into light as white
as though the prisms
were not there.

BIRDSONG

Messiaen captured whistles,
warbles in his net of notes,
trapped them with five-lined
staffs, transforming
fleeting sounds into
thrilling songs, fixed,
until, as composers do,
as poets do, he quavered
the finite black on white
into strange rhythms,
lyrical movements,
altered instruments
so musicians and devotees
must adjust to new
experiences, enjoyment
enhanced by differences.

Permanent goes
impermanent
one more time.

BITTERSWEET

Joy and a smile at the start of a trailhead,
helped over a boulder by a strong man's hand,
his muscled arm fuzzy with dark hair.
Sierra Nevada high mountain odors, dust
and sap, bird tweets matched to the altitude,
tenacious mounds of yellow snow we passed
with a steady stride. We balanced rock to rock
over giardia-polluted streams, creels and packs
filled with worms, shiny-red salmon eggs,
smelly green-gold floating bait.
Gripping flexible rods, minds semi-focused
on possible action, we watched swift dark clouds
gather behind Bloody Mountain, Morrison Peak,
breathed sweet and deep, unafraid of the trail back.

Years later,
above the Alto Adige, from funicular to funicular,
we followed pretzeling trails, saw an edelweiss
(miniscule bloom with overblown reputation),
pairs of British, like red-cheeked round birds
wearing matching pants, jackets, packs, backs
straight, push off on their trekking. Germans
in leather boots, short pants (not lederhosen)
passed a French group, blanket spread over
flat terrain, an al fresco tasting of cheeses,
sausages, wine. Nearer home than we were,
smiling at us, they waved farewell.

Today, in the Santa Monicas, a hike rated
by miles, elevation gain, steepness of trails
draws a small group of a certain age, worn
boots, brimmed hats, sunscreen, gloves,
water bottles on belts, armed with hiking
sticks for balance, support. Strong male hands,
well-muscled arms are gone long ago.
A few hours hike, then lunch, cars parked

close to the trailhead, preserving energy.

As hikers falter, vanish from the trails,
from the troop, each warns me,
Do not hike alone,
never hike alone.

BLACK ICE

If tires could tiptoe,
   mine would
by pines tall at attention,
by rocks, unexpected in release
from cliffside confinement,
hiding sharp spears
behind the highway skirts.

This is an alien place,
unmarked spaces of slick,
   invisible black ice,
a possible skid
into an arc, airborne
toward a rimmed river.

In my mind I envision
this dark water
as a ribbon of film,
still in negative form,
hypnotic in its continuity,
its repetition.

That scene imprinted
   on my eye, I swerve.

BLACKBERRIES

Each separate lobe of every berry
pushes at the membrane that dams the juice,
released when bitten into
or when squeezed
or punctured by its own thorny twig.

I am eager for the pleasure
of a gush from the wild
into my tame mouth. I thrust
my hands into the thicket,
grab berries; my arms
are scratched, skin laid open.

The juice stains my fingers,
paints my palm with a symbol,
a faux port wine mark; I'm afraid
it's a sign of misfortune.

Some berries taste bitter to me.
Some are dried out; the season
has passed. Their maidenhead
taken, discarded fruit husks
litter the ground. I struggle
with my impatience, my lack
of faith. Wait for next year's crop.

BRISTLECONES

Gnarled, with trunks and limbs twisted
by winds that batter their high mountain
retreat, desiccate the desert below,
bristlecones cling to the thin soil,
models, for us, of prized longevity.

Paiutes came here to gather nuts
from the pinons at lower elevations.
They used fallen limbs for fires,
travelled on foot or horseback,
respectful of the trees, already old.

Nutcrackers and blue Steller's jays
override the whistling wind
with raucous cries, searching
for a few scattered seeds.
Sun-loving chipmunks flirt
their tails, earn crusts from visitors.

Booted hikers come in jeeps
with four-wheel drive, try to get
as close as they can to the trailhead.
An occasional biker roars up,
looking for the road to Deep Springs.
A family in a SUV wants
a picnic spot for kids and dogs.

Under branches stripped of bark, crunching
as they walk on pumice pebbles, people
leave offerings for these ancient trees,
of wrappers, metal pull-tops,
Styrofoam, and the lingering
smell of emission incense.

BY LUNDY LAKE

red fir/white fir
misshapen rectangle,
last year's, ranger-made blaze
for tenderfeet like me.
Downed branches, light snow
but extreme winds, natural
occurrences impact, like falling
stars on vision, ageing joints
on not-so-firmly planted feet.

Woodsmen define location,
limit wandering. I wish for
roaming below fluttering leaves,
pointed sharp limbs, dry needles.
Lower aspen, water-seeking willows,
already yellow, shiver, proclaim
the season's end, the falling
under cold rain, white flakes.

My spirit's testing, learning,
growth is not ended yet.
Oxygen replenishes my blood,
my reasons to rise in early morning,
seek wider challenges, brush up
heart, brain. More stages of man
to come after shrunk shanks,
and I must be included in one.

No matter how much I walk with
birdsong under the forest canopy,
I sense the rapid pulse
of creatures scurrying to store
bits of green, wild grain.
I do not have will enough, force enough
to circumscribe the cycle.
It takes world's end to snap the universe.

BELLS

Tiny bells tinkle,
drowned out by hefty ones.
Air currents force a surf
of clamor, boisterous
and painful to the ears,
a Sunday song of guilt
to stay-at-home parishioners.

Nearer than the buoy bells,
swaying on choppy waters,
warning sailors and seals
of danger ahead, are bells
that sing of triumphs,
hide the harsher tones,
cover discord with harmony.

Wise men, conquerors
of deafness can hear
the ugly reluctant
alarms hidden from us
by the bell ringers.

CHICAGO

City of taxis,
skirting the winding canyons
between ponderous buildings seen
from the river as phallic spires,
so a female architect erected one
with a vaginal, slit rooftop
to balance all that testosterone.

The river, like most world rivers,
flows filthy gray, embellished by soggy cups,
plastic boxes, except that, unlike the Ganges,
there are no bloated bodies of cows here,
and no one wants a souvenir bottle of this water.

My son and I walk by monuments to finance
and, fronting them on sidewalks,
the stubby pylons, rectangular, scattered
between asphalt and entrances, silent
pillars preventing trucks filled
with explosives from obliterating
the business center, and,
incidentally, murdering people.

Chicago has shifted from Sandburg's
hog butchers to the nation, builders
of railroads, skyscrapers open to all,
to screening everyone who would enter,
trusting no one, so focused
on terrorists, so fearful of bombs.

Millennium Park, the Bean, the fountains, an art
museum tour, then an overview from the 104th
floor of the Willis building, the only way
to glimpse Lake Michigan, and up here
a spider occupying its web, living isolated
in silence above the rush, the roar.

CONTINENTS

lag in slow drift, plate laps plate,
shelf slides an inch or less
this past year of bullets, plowing
rows into tough turf, forcing
lead, iron, copper back
into their origins, buried again.

Rocky clods bombed high
fall back as hail, hard,
stoning the violators, the innocents.
Murdered flesh decays, enriches
soil six feet down into earth's mantle.

The deep core, sluggish, boiling,
never fields incoming bullets.
The rant of blistering souls,
cells from hell, has no effect.
Pillars of smoke arise,

become clouds that rag out,
drift over the altering planet.
Plate laps plate, shelf slides
an inch or less,
this looming year of bullets,
strafing channels into tough turf.

CORMORANTS

A storm crashes waves
over the breakwater. If I
were out there, I'd be dashed
against the stone wall,
drowned, unlike the cormorant.
He is the CEO of sea birds.

With no rights of possession
in the breakwater, he perches
on top of it as though he owned
each stone and, lacking self-restraint,
ices the rocks with white
trickles of guano.

He dives daily, fishing only
for himself, keeps his entire
catch. In America, no one
makes him share.
In Japan and other places,
he might dive for a master.

Satiated, he lounges in the sun,
spreads his wings wide,
puffs his chest out.
His body seems to grow.
He looks impressive, inspires
his chicks, as well as curlews
and sandpipers, mere shore birds.

He chases a quarry away from
other hunters, or surf fishermen,
downs it in a hurry, flies off,
leaving any followers
to fish for themselves.

DAY HIKE

Outdoors again, at last, after days of rain
(or aches and pains), we cross a swollen creek
balancing in our heavy-soled boots
from stone to stone. The red-dirt trail,
eroded by the water into puckered ridges,
rises up to edge the cliff top.

Down the bluff sides, tufts of bushes beard the slopes:
ceanothus with its fragile, lilac plumes,
sumac, sturdy, its tenacious roots galvanized
        to hold the soil.
buckwheat, white and popeyed, sending out seeds,
        building family.

We toss anecdotes between us as we climb:
        the day park rangers spent searching for a hiker
        who had gone home, telling no one;
        the day the hornets chased us down a mountain,
        furious, stinging as they flew.

We trade adventure tales:
        African safaris, helicopter hikes in Canada,
        bicycling in Europe, trekking in Nepal.

We exchange family news:
        son, daughter, in-law tales, more often now
        it's grandkids, their achievements and their goals.

We wonder where some hikers are that haven't joined us
for some time.

Under an early spring sun we bend forward,
plodding up the trail, testing calves and
quadriceps against the push.
We search for shade, stop, raise our bottles,
let the water trickle down our throats,

celebrate our gain,
replenish what we've lost.

DAY SAIL

Wind whistling strong, steady as it blows,
filling sails, fast clip, port side down,
dipping toward deep water—I don't want to know
what lies far below—bouncing over chop,
wake of passing power boat, motors retching as it goes,
I yell to be heard, share excitement, wishing
I had grown up with boats, as some here
have, so I could help with spilling, catching
wind, pushing knot speed up—oh, my,
we're doing sixteen!—flying high on
starboard I search the sea, wishing for a
pilot whale, dolphin, exotic bird, something
for me to offer as a gift to the skipper, the
helmswoman. I am here enjoying
the racing, bouncing freedom of wind and
sea; the boat sucking greedily at full sails,
then down, then up again, loving the body
of shine, splatter and just a frisson, at
the cold spray. This little boat is
smooth in the chop, even when we turn to
head back around the buoy. We are
exhilarated; let's do this again soon;
skipper is willing and so we all are.
This small ephemeral family of friends,
five in a pod, spills out onto the dock.
The family disperses, each single again.

DEER IN SUNLIGHT

step out on stilt-like legs,
knobby knees flex,
hesitant hooves tip-toe.
Soft doe eyes watch
the white-spotted
following fawns as hidden
young watchers, gasp
and giggle *ooh-ooh*.

Beyond the bucolic scene,
their forests diminishing,
deer bed down on dry branches.
   A sharp twig mattress
   pokes hard into old bones,
   joints creak on dawn rising,
   shake on first standing.

Nostrils point up,
seeking to scent danger.
Threats sniffed before
eyes or ears reveal
any villainy, teach
them beyond intelligence.

Vision clouds, hearing
fades, age steals acuity.
They know what they knew at birth—
   recoil from sudden motions,
   tremble at a footfall,
   a swish of air
   beyond familiar boundaries.

QUARTET

The face of the cellist twists,
his brow wrinkles, his mouth
tenses, permits a wry smile.
Bartok began this quartet
faced with failure, despair.
I hear pain in his chords.

Music surges
through the room.
The movement ends.
We stand, applaud
the musicians, bestow
the approval every artist
craves—*bravo! bravo!*

Persistent violins, viola join
the cello. Passionate phrases
plead for the acceptance, the acclaim
his homeland denied the composer
when it condemned him
to die in an alien land.

CAPSULES

Robert Schumann died 100 years after Mozart's birth.

Continuo, on a small keyboard,
an instrument delicate
in color and structure
for an age reluctant to change,
in a tempo paced
for a minuet or a mazurka
to keep the rhythm
of the eighteenth century
from spilling over
into phrasing unknown,
suspect.

Violins, familiar curves,
strung with catgut,
played with horsehair bows,
hammered brass horns,
wood or metal flutes,
the old instruments
for the old music,
applauded by the audience
with grey heads bobbing.

*The Grateful Dead plays together for the first
time in the ten years since Jerry died.*

Amplifiers.
Metal reflects stage strobes,
red floods
over the spectrum,

booms into the twenty-first century.
The keyboard,
sleek, is carried
onto the stage,
plastic, black, and shiny.
Guitars with silver frets
are danced around,
strapped onto barely covered
torsos.

Band members bounce,
skitter back and forth,
yell into hand-held,
puff-headed mikes
(an abundance of notes?)
barely heard above the din,
drums and cymbals vibrate.
The audience bounds,
screams,
waving arms,
shaking bodies,
swishing hair
dyed green, blue, purple,
hair strands sparkling.

ENDURANCE

Sounds, phrases evoke
            Coltrane or Monk,
                        classics replayed
                                    by combos no longer
                        sleek tigers but old
            cats hanging out,
paws poised over
            keys and valves.
                        We know the riffs,
                                    the bridges,
                        sway our torsos,
            snap our fingers
in this lounge
            where the crowd
                        nurses one beer
                                    to last the night,
                        swings legs over knees
            to jazz revisited.

JAZZ IN THE FOREST

Guitar twangs, split by trees, thread through needles
of pine and fir, insinuate into the ears of the mostly
middle-aged folks slouched in plastic chairs.

Wawooms of trumpets push paths around trees,
blurt into the ears of roadies, wearing primary-
colored tees labeled with their band's name, logo.

Bwamps of trombones, *blouches* of saxes plunge
through underbrush, through hanging dead fronds, crawl
into the ears of jazz fans, settle for a few sets.

Drums boom, cymbals clash, bumble back
through ears into minds, connecting
the rhythm through thigh bones to foot bones.

Bridges go to elsewhere, riffs chase them home,
wrap up, deliver whole phrases into eight-beat
piano boogies, slowing into blues. A jazz singer

a big woman, mellows the air with lyrics whispering
of romance, broken hearts, familiar tunes that cry
a river over youth gone, lovers gone, and the mood

turns dark. I relive my memories, my losses,
applaud the talent, breathe deep and sigh.

ENERGY

White chemical deposits adjoin
green pools where earth's insides
boil to the surface, releasing odorous
gasses. Prick a bubble. The smell
of rotten eggs tells you where you are—
Yellowstone, Rotorua, Iceland.
          Building thermal energy—
                    useful, but not enough.

Rivers rush headlong, gulping water
into whirlpools, forcing out waterfalls
into deeps behind dams, energizing
turbines to create power—light
to fight darkness and fear;
communications—to talk to each
each other, watch each other;
          water power—
                    good, but not enough.

Greedy, we need more, more, faster.
We must exceed nature, search for new
energy—reach up, reach down.
Up we find wind, sunlight, clean.
          Slow.
Down, we find coal to burn, gas to burn,
pollution to make eyes smart, lungs cough and spew.
          Fast.

DEAL OF YOUR LIFE!

Masons wearing visored caps
plug every stone-edged space.
Even Pyramus and Thisbe
couldn't find an opening
through which to cement
their plot. A mixer grinds
and crunches, spews out mortar,
spatters the workmen's boots.

From mixer to wheelbarrow
to trowel to rock,
the masons bend, lift, twist
to the beat of the machine,
the rhythm a kick to the ass,
a punch to the arm.
The wall rises.

From over the structure,
a radio blasts out
country music, shakes down
lyrics into repetition
punctuated by metronome beats
of amplified banjos and guitars.

Every fifteen minutes, a voice
interrupts with station ID,
with bargains on autos,
TVs, or washing machines—
" . . . no down payment
 . . . interest free for . . .
 . . . a limited offer, grab it today
deal of your life . . . "

FARMER'S MARKET

In this place, on this planet
munched on by humans,
strides a produce-seeker.
Her neck, creped, wattled,
swivels, eyes peer,
ears hear the hawking—
fullness of oranges,
sweetness of tangerines,
strange heirlooms, tawny,
green-striped tomatoes
not bred to be red.
Exotics today—golden beets, purple potatoes, black radishes,
appetite boosters for the overfed.
Flowers—backyard sunflowers to hothouse orchids,
no scents from either.
There are no bees;
shoppers are wary of bees.

Organic lettuce shelters gleeful
insects, lucky in their choice
of farmer. He owns,
in exchange, a smug smirk
as he prances before
his anti-pesticidal
canvas sign. But
his boxes are plastic, his bags—
those drain-clogging,
fence-attacking,
rag-tags banned in other countries

FISH STORY

A line is thrown out.
A thin, transparent, tough filament
that snarls around itself
and any hooked fish.
It must be reeled in fast
before the hook tears into guts,
bloodies the captive.

Old line, brittle, breaks
with little pressure from fingers
uncut by strands spinning fast
and tight off the spool.
Stretched line wimps out,
fiddles into curls relaxed
like worn-out springs.

A lure is cast out, inedible,
fools worm-eaters into chasing
base metal that glints gold, silver
as it bounces through bottom grass.
Fish fate rests on the speed
of its dash, the depth
of its hunger and experience.

The line slackens, the fish spits
the hook, twitches away, blurring
the line with muddy ripples.
When the fish's tale is spun,
it too will blur from mere
catchable into a great cannibal
capable of dining off its young.

FISHING

I fish and my fingers finesse
the small activities. I lob a lead
weight high, plop it into water, wait,
line taut, for a soft-mouthed tug.

No one stands behind me,
not anymore, but I sense
footfalls. Only the crunch
remains to complete the stride,
wide in lug-soled boots.

When I catch up,
he had moved on,
skirting the gravelly shallows,
searching for the perfect pool,
fish concealed in swirls.
Restless, he sought the finer
configuration of the stream.

I trail, plumb with patience
his rejected whirlpools. Playing
into riffles, bouncing
off moss-smooth rocks, I find
what he missed,
stick my catch in my creel.

FLOATING WORLDS

Breath forced through pursed
lips floats the bubbles
high, rising away,
dripping with suds.
The bubbles blush
pink-to-violet
tints that slide across
the skin of the spheres
as I follow,
focused on their
translucent shapes.

Air alone can move them,
my touch too solid
to shepherd such delicacy.
One by one they break,
vanish, leave space
emptier than it was
before they were here.
The pastel rainbow
disappears with them,
and I miss it
for the rest of the day.

FOG

Brilliant,
lidded by a shifting,
tattered chiffon of fog,

the opalescent sphere
commands my gaze.

This sun,
so moonlike in its glow,
does not
stamp a green impression
on my naked retina.

Sun
drops toward a swallowing sea.

Fog
has sucked the brightness from the day.

FORCE OF NATURE

Wind frills the slender palm
fronds that alter the face of gardens;
the trees bend, flexible, bow
to the strong force, bounce up again,
a bowstring released, a graceful snap
up, tossing their manes like racing foals.

It's the stiff ones, branches
breaking, shredding
in the teeth of the gale, that
crack, crash to hard
ground, fracture into kindling,
not suitable for much else.

Roots dismembered, a hole appears,
witness to loss of a growing
thing ripped away, no longer
remembered, not even by the earth.

FIRE GARDEN

Sumac and manzanita thrust black finger
bones upward, sketching a silhouette
of broken lines. Scorched bark peels off
in strips, revealing, by a pumpkin
orange core, a Halloween of colors.
Blistered shrubs stand naked, green
shoots of grass sprouting like hair
in their root hollows.

Lilac lupines, cream and lavender
Mariposa lilies, pink patches of
prickly phlox, vermillion poppies,
small, red spears of paintbrush
fill in the spaces, outline the rocks.

They had all been there before,
forced to bow to powerful big brothers
of bushes and trees that guzzled
the sunlight, leaving shadows for
the flowers, lying stillborn or
sterile in their darkened beds.
Now sun shines through stripped
branches, warming the seed
and the bulbs, pulling newborn
flowers into a charred landscape.

Burrows in the henna earth make
mounds where subterranean
creatures, sweltering under hellish
flame, dug ever deeper trying to
survive. Those who fled returned
to reopen ash-clogged tunnels and
descend into underground nests.

The people, cars overloaded with
possessions, had driven with heads

shrouded in clouds of smoke,
sucking it into their lungs.
Their skulls about to burst from
heat and fear, their bodies weighted
down as though with boulders,
they moved as in a dream while
firefighters screamed,

"Save yourselves. Forget your things."
Seizing on pain to gain strength,
they hurled boxes of photographs
onto auto seats or into trunks.
Minds cannot be trusted to replicate
the images of family now changed,
or friends of long ago.

"Save the photos. They are important!"

Some looked back and saw their memories
shaved thin, curling into black skins
as though they were still alive.
Shivering, they watched years vanish
into cinders. Silent, drenched in
sweat, they sheltered each other.
Some snatched paintings, trinkets,
jewels, broken toys, fur coats,
and carried them and kept on running.

Now the hills are covered with a
patchwork quilt of shades and
shapes in a kaleidoscope of colors.
Seen scattered through the blooms
are piles of tumbled bricks,
rusted metal, crushed Spanish roof
tiles. Of different texture, they share
the same sanguine color and,
alongside, the straight lines
of blackened stumps.

WILDFIRE

Cooker of food, cleanser of rot,
warmer of the unsheltered, fire
ran amok among clumps
of desiccated sage, creosote
bushes, raged across the highway,
browning big cottonwoods
along a spindly creek,
burning through one
somber day, one red night.

Burnt earth rivals the blackness
of lava outcroppings. Devastated
piedmont fans soften under
grey ash deep in places
where smoke plumes rise,
spiraling upwards today.

Tomorrow—thin, persistent.

CRUEL APRIL

The breeze, deceptive,
turns cold without
warning, twisting leaves,
chilling their newborn
greenness.

Old branches, skeletonized
by winter, poke their
mocking brown bones
through fresh foliage.

Escape, one more time, for a
few months, into a world
where limbs stretch wide to
welcome the sun's blessing.

Tingle with anticipation.
Touch buds that are firm,
that thrust into the air with
promises of ripe openings.

Those that keep that promise
will unfold into soft pastels
or rainbow brilliance.

Those that break that promise
will shrivel into fragile
dryness, carpeting the
ground with added husks.

FROZEN WATERFALL

Flowing down
or bouncing up,
sudden freeze
grips the water.

Downward falling
drops pull, push,
vector off, to slant
towards least resistance.
I must follow, slide
in the wake of others.

Upward rising, I imagine
feisty drops, striking
against trends, spitting
into the face of formality,
strong enough to leap
over curling foam
onto a divergent path,
pull away from the crowd.

I touch the icicles lightly,
fear my fingers might
stick. I feel chilled.
My hands, my face prickly,
frosty skin tight. The
caress of a warm hand
on my face is painful.

HAIKUS

Ear-splitting thunder
     flaming lightning
          rain wears down the stones

Summer's end
     bare rose hips
          lost fragrance

Cloud shadow patterns
     ripple over ridges
          a patchwork quilt

An infant's wail
     mother, food, caresses
          loneliness

The unlit, twisted path
     not dark enough
          to fool the owl

Two roads cross
     one can choose
          to read signs

Wings barely still
     a poised butterfly
          tastes salt on my hand

Heron guards a pool
     its coiled neck, snake-like
          a sudden release

An empty plate
     the straw bird bows its head
          and eats

Wallowing in muck
　　　　the frog goggles—swallows—
　　　　　　　　a delicate fly

Wind blows down
　　　　a cooling chimney, stirs up heat
　　　　　　　　from ashes

Poised on a lofty post
　　　　the hawk watches
　　　　　　　　an odd clump of earth

Full moon, cloud-free sun
　　　　either is
　　　　　　　　dangerous

A woman of a certain age
　　　　walks by the sea
　　　　　　　　it washes her feet

Squawking crows complain
　　　　of meager compensation
　　　　　　　　for accomplishment

Red and pink rosebuds
　　　　white lilies bound in a wreath
　　　　　　　　beginning and end

THE HIKE

Stay here and wait for me!
There is no path that we can swing down
hand in hand, only a narrow way with room for one.
Poison!
Triple green leaves fuse into a warning red fringe.
Caution!
Fingers of unburied roots loop to make traps.
Danger!
Exposed rocks slant their hard sides out of hazardous walls.

Leaves drift into yellow patches
stitched with white puffs of cottonwood
outlined by brown burrs of sycamore.
Flowers swirl around boulders fringing them
with red, white, purple curtains that sway
to the tread of my feet. Birds
whistle absurd notes. I have
no time for interpretation.
I pass it by, this natural beauty,
rushing down, bound for the creek-smoothed rocks
that glisten with a wet welcome,
licked by the water,
the water that wrinkles my reflection
crowning a strong body with an old woman's face.

This water is not refreshing: it is sick with
pollution. Undrinkable. I have brought
my own and I gulp it down.
Looking upward, I see the bluff high above
oozing a liquid. The cliff is leaking, leaving
streaks that dry brown in the hot sun.

I must go back, sweating as I struggle
upward, hands gripping rocks
to pull myself up. I have no choice.
My mind forces me on. I cannot tell

from below if there is someone up
above who still waits for me.

THE MONASTERY TREE

Down below, through the mist,
rises the monastery tree.
It is decked with random ovals,
empty spaces, cowled by fringes
of dark-veined leaves.

A few bare branches reinforce
the emptiness, furnishing the ovals
with sparse, drought-dried twigs.
The foliage droops in resignation.

Blossomless   Fruitless

A shell of brown bark is shrouded
by grey tatters of cobwebs, relics
of disappointed spiders.
Birds sneak a furtive snack in
the shadows below the leaves.
Carcass eaters lurk in this
dreary diner.

Wind whistles the fog mist
into a sleety shower. The
bare twigs and scrawny
branches shift and crack in
the mounting cold under the
tattered protection of the
leaves of the monastery tree.

I ABHOR HOLES

there's one now—I need to act.
A space once seen can't be ignored.
I grab a small canary pine, a six-incher, pop
it in the center, give dirt-encrusted roots
a chance to grow. It stands absurdly straight,
a tiny staunchness vying strong against the drag
and tug of life. No pampering now, no
weakening of its native strength. Water
just enough and leave it on its own.

A few days pass, no sprint of growth,
too soon, but a few days more and then
a week, and I begin to doubt its hardiness.
It may have borne within itself a serious
disease from insects or insidious worms.

I have no room in my orderly,
circumscribed garden for failure
to thrive. I will not blame myself.
It had its chance, but now I see it
shriveled, yellowed, dried.

A new hole appears.

IF A SURVIVOR IS FOUND, PLEASE CALL

Air currents eddied, sucked up water,
wrapped it in ferocious winds,
smashed it onto levees, churches,
homes, all the frailties that make
us better than Noah's beasts.

Snatching a glance at the emerging sun,
some saw on closed eyelids a white
splotchy glare oozing into purple tinged
with green, like a bruise on the skin,
and pleaded with an unrepentant heaven.

Some perished of thirst, swimming
beside corpses, even of children,
who might have floated on splintered
boards, but feared leaving, losing family.

The spinning earth threw off
a smashing blow, destroyed
the poorest among us, believers
or not in any one of many gods,
using weapons as deadly as those
invented by the tribes of man.

IN TRAINING

Tossing a mane,
hoofs pawing the earth,
rolling eyes unfocused,
watchful for suspicious moves
by humans wielding nooses
threatening to tighten
around the equine throat,
breath shortening, neck
twisting, my tender
nose points downward
headed for pebbly dirt.

Stay away human, ponder—
how would you take
to having me mount your back
and dig my hoofs into your
stomach? I know what's coming.

You will insist I follow orders,
hits there—rewards here,
bribery and cudgel
alternating. I will comply
or miss my carrot treats,
my oats served in a nose bag.

If I strike back,
kick a hoof out
to collide with a tender spot,
buck a rider to the ground
and run away
with a happy neigh,
I will be punished.

Been like this for centuries,
deviation discouraged,
brilliant innovation stymied,

unless the human in charge
sees his own profit in it.

LACE CURTAINS

Workers swelter in subtropical
heat, monitor tatting machines
that strive to exceed
the world's demand for lace:
lace for curtains, genteel,
not-so-genteel curtains,
middle-class curtains that close off
from furtive eyes the nakedness
of those who can choose
to dance in secluded interiors.

A dancer whirls, arms outstretched,
abandoned to the moment,
able to swirl up a breeze, spinning
it off her body, pushing it through
the open window,
rippling out the curtain
in successive parallel waves.

A viewer outside perceives
light, not the dancer's
face, the pride glowing there,
hidden behind the lace.
So much prettier than burlap,
so much more refined,
her hard-earned salary
bought her reward.
Lace curtains bring her
a cut above.

LOOKING WESTWARD

from the Pacific shore, distant
breakers undulating like a huge wet chest,
sucking in, pumping out,
he stands unaware
of anything behind him.

What is not seen is best forgotten.
What is forgotten excuses him
from a litany of murmured memories.

The roar and hiss
of tumbling pebbles
fill ears that are deaf
to ghetto blasters,
screaming kids,
whistling parents.

He wraps up in a towel
of separation,
staring,
        moving
toward the sheltering sea.

LOW TIDE

My feet imprinted in wet sand
fill as water bubbles upward,
disappear as I move,
alarming the small sandpipers,
their tiny fairy-like bodies too
light to indent the surface,
ballet in the wash, forming chorus
lines, pecking at invisible mites,
swinging from the left side
all the way to the right,
still in formation, still dancing
with persistent foam
flecks and the rising tide.

MARY, MARY

Night whitens, the fog decays,
plants limp, black, soggy,
creep out to be seen
as stringy, yellowed stems
of crab grass. Wimpy bow-legged
stalks of wannabe roses, just
a shade too common,
still stubbornly occupy
their ground, prepare

to push out weeds, save
the garden from spray gun-
wielding ploughmen
determined to eliminate
occupiers, defenders of
common wheat and rye,
the sharers of fertile soil,
even the lowly
but necessary earthworms.

The wannabes, fenced
off from prospering, from blooming,
fend off ploughmen who withhold
life-giving water, even for
restoration of the ailing, the broken.

Reaching out tendrils,
wannabes seek new growths
alike enough to strengthen
each other, occupying
more plots, reseeding
constantly to be tough,
jungle-like, prepared
to overwhelm the great
machines of the ploughmen.

MOMENT

The plan:
tread the dirt path,
traipse through trees,
circle sparse wildflower patches,
spend twilight at the brook.

Semi-dark closes in,
shadows stain the light,
sharp-edged sight line
blurs, he stumbles.

From his hand, a rimmed oblong
smacks hard against cracked earth,
crazing the concave surface
into a reflecting jigsaw puzzle.

A tumble steals time from a day,
draws it close
around nursing of bruises,
soothing of aches.

A fraction of a second,
a person,
an object,
a plan,
altered for all time.

MOONLESS NIGHT

In the clearing before
the high mountain cabin,
I tilt my head way back.
The night sky is a pointillist
painting, white sparkles,
thicker at the Milky Way.

Dark tops of pines and firs,
ragged spears around
the rim of a domed hollow,
frame, tonight, what ancients
saw—stars stuck on the base
of an inverted bowl
that covered the world.

Constellations shimmer, pulsate.
Orion, macho hunter, threatens
to control the heavens. Cassiopeia,
queenlike on her throne, refuses
to yield. Too late for reconciliation,

I concede the heavens to them, study
the empty cabin, the clouds from
my breath. It has taken me years
to come here alone to grieve, face
all the memories. I hear no life sounds
coming from the woods. I shiver,
my raised face wet in the silence.

MUSEUM VISIT

The room is heavy
with German Expressionism:
Pechstein, Dix, Max Beckmann's people
outlined in black, thick with anguish.
Here is the Kathe Kollwitz woodcut—a circle
of women, arms wrapped round each other
for comfort and support.

I stood before this drawing once, with him,
arms linked, hips touching,
until the open mouths of the Kollwitz women,
their slumped postures, their neediness,
made us aware of our own bodies,
hurried us off to a nearby hotel.

Mourning for the passionate
look in his eyes drew me here,
not to the memorial
his family had arranged.

The women in this drawing
died in sorrow years ago.
The museum, nearly deserted,
is dirtier than I remember,
the picture frame marred,
the paper dingier,
the glass more scratched.

I shiver as the sound
of heels on the wooden
floor carries
on the chilled air.

NIGHTMARE

Run and run, panic
my wits gather,
shove me
over the wall.

Reason splattered its shell
against that wall,
its yellow center
runs over my fingers,
makes me pluck

the stain,
the chain of fractal
islands, green
on brown camouflage

confounds hunters,
deaf, unthinking,
I kowtow
before apocalyptic
riders,

surrounded,
mounded under clouds,
dust coverlets,
a sudden kick,
I escape,
startled, gasp,
reborn
into my world.

NO ALBATROSS HERE

Ignored,
the foghorn's hollow
bellow warns

              breakwater here,
              channel entrance,
              no GPS, skipper aware
              he can't blame an albatross.

No albatross here,
pelicans, yes, surface skimmers
pouch puffed sideways
by onshore winds, head
shoreward, vanish in darkness—
              Don't follow them!

CHOOSE

Shoeless, grab preservers,
jump toward the unseen
beach where gulls gloat,
windswept on the sand,
heads, tucked.
              Let the boat founder

OR

Pocket all watches,
jewelry, cash, cell phones,
claw the wheel
with a death grip

              shudder into reverse.
              struggle into the wind

PRAY.

ON LEAVING THE BEACH

Reluctantly, she retrieves the sieve,
pail, shovel so they will not be
pulled into an undertow, dragged
out, forced into the floating plastic
sea, the below-surface layer,
toxic curse to ocean's tiny
life, or so the grown-ups claim.

Now to sandals so foot soles
don't burn from hotter sand
or cement sidewalks or
asphalt streets. Dragging
those feet, she regrets the loss
of low-tide footprints squishing
in saturated sand, scattered
feathers of gulls and terns,
bits of shell discovered while
digging, even detritus of
uncertain origin that makes
mothers scream, *Put that down!*

Shy, she tugs at the elastic
around her bottom; she clears
out the sand from her
ruffled one-piece suit.

No tears now, we'll be back
soon. Unless, of course,
impediments arise.

ON RETURNING TO THE BEACH

My nipples perk erect, not passion
but icy wind, surf-delivered
that sweeps across my breasts, cheats
them of sand-secreted warmth.

The towel I splayed out on,
face downward, sun-glassed
and sun-screened,
now becomes my cape,
an uneven drapery, but enough
to conquer goose flesh,
my nipples into softness.

Tides, pulled more by the moon
than I am, generate the waves'
continuous roil, the motion that
lulls with its gravel-choked
roar, the white noise that blurs

into dark summer nights,
a deserted beach,
stripping down to dash
into phosphorescent foam,
out to wrap up together,
sharing our warmth
in one blanket.

Only a few isolated bodies
sun today in October, past
the prime of summer. I wrap up
tighter, stand, drag my low
chair, stagger off, lurching
sideways over ever-shifting sand.

It used to be easy.

PERFORMANCE SPACE[3]

Mud hens line up, swim
in formation across the channel.

Beak to tail, they ripple the surface,
now a semblance of skeletal ribs,
backbone, some extinct creature.

The birds angle back, their wake
draws into puckers, a healing
scar on the skin of the water.

The designs they create move
with them until a small
motor launch bears down.

The birds scatter. The pattern
that flowed from them riffles
into turbulence. Many minutes
pass before the water's surface
regains the calm, the peace.

---

3   Published in *California Quarterly*, Vol 30, No. 3. 2004.

PERSONAL GAMES

In hijab or manteau I couldn't leap
a hurdle, swim a medley, dive
for a volleyball where a body splits
the space between the ball and ground.

In jilbab I could not dance ballet.
Pirouettes need pink tights, tutus,
arms that lift with grace beside
even pinker cheeks that glow.

In chador I couldn't roller blade.
Long skirts tangle, I would crash
in pain and blood. Injuries heal,
but my will to play would die.

I don't wear hijab or manteau,
but my mind is cloaked. I can't
seem to find some answers, make
a choice, begin a love affair.
Frozen, I await an outside force
to strip away the veil, release
me from a claustrophobic
burqa, enable me to act.

POPULATION GROWTH[4]

In his designated hollow,
where the beach is darker,
less patrolled, a man,
cocooned in a grimy
orange sleeping bag curls
up over his midden of glass
and paper, pulls an old
shirt over his nose and mouth.

Sand sounds like a zipper
as it slides over his black
plastic bag full of treasures.
More sand drizzles down
his face as he wakes from
fearful naps, watches sun
rise through reddened eyes.

Sitting up, he looks around,
sees other mounds, yards
away from each other,
half-buried homeless
people. More arrive
every day, intruding
into his territory.

4   Published in *California Quarterly*, Vol. 30, No. 4. 2005.

MOUNTAIN LION

Alarmists warn of a mountain lion
in the neighborhood. Lacking country
prey, it stalks things separated, weak:
dogs, cats, children, anyone alone.
I am full-grown, but I fear the cat.

Beneath live oaks, I look up to search
green-furred branches where a shape
might lean against the trunk to sharpen
claws. I walk trails deep into chaparral,
eyeing the ledges, watching for movement
that will isolate a different shade of brown.
The cat's nocturnal, but the shrouded sun
that casts so many shadows on short winter
days, might lure it from its den to sit on
tawny haunches, looking over the
off-road pathways where I wander.

Experts tell us not to run, movement alarms the beast.
I do not trust myself to stand and wait alone
while eyes, restless, yellow, measure weakness.
It is smart to set out traps, to drug the bait,
being careful not to lick my fingers, not become
addicted to the drug or snare myself.

I have faced this mountain lion before, his scarred
face, his forepaw with a ripped-off patch of skin.
He is a coward who runs away from many.
Two can make him hesitate and turn.
One alone can only hide behind closed eyes.
The lion seems to disappear.
But when the eyes reopen and no one
else is there, he will return.

PUDDLES

Rain blisters the skin of a puddle,
pushes it out of its paramecium
shape, edged with a tiny hair-like
fringe, but the edges dissolve,
muddied, dirt-dark, pitted by hard
drops of water, always on the move.

Hollows in the cement become
water-filled nests for twigs that fall,
scabbed from leaf loss, needing
some place to be held. Rain
pushes twigs around, floats leaves,
runs through the channels
that divide the sidewalk,
except where it is cracked,
releasing a tiny cascade.

Rain over, the water's surface
reflects a tree trunk, the mottled
gray of the sky. Breeze ripples
the reflections into iron-colored
fragments. The water, slow
to abandon its position, recedes,
coats the hollow with torn
leaves and curled up bodies
of worms caught unprepared.

QUIET WORK

Siren-like metal saws whine across pipe,
          table saws buzz the board's length.

Staple guns chunk into insulation. Hammers
          drive through air lubricated by the memory of muscles.

Silences are rests to rectify errors, chat, question,
          blow away slivers and chips.

Foremen measure jobs half-done. Time oversees the settlement.
Clock hands drag around the circle, shadowing the sun's progress.
Order rules, A precedes B, both before C.

Building from the top down, a metaphor for some
          deeper dream, cherished thought,
leads downward to seeds of creation,
          grown with mental sweat, even anguish.

SAN FERNANDO VALLEY, HERE I COME

I perch on an asphalt outcropping, the smog
ceiling hovers below me, above the
valley floor. Looking up, walkers see blue
through brown; looking down, I see
glittering car roofs, almost connected,
form multi-colored scales, snake up, down,
around the black lines of the grid, chase
the tail of the car in front, seek the mouse
in the house, or office, or school, win prime
parking, save five commuter minutes.

The valley floor writhes with movement;
cars, buses, bikes, walkers, all destination
bound. I want to leap down, join them.
I don't know where they are heading,
have no place I am bound to get to.
My fierce urge is to tear down the hill,
leap into the action, join them, now!

SILENT IN GREYNESS

They inhabit the surf line, floaters
on winking wavelets. Surfers,
mounded into the child's pose,
quiet for a time, move to paddle
their boards into new currents.

Between surface and bottom
hovers a sleek animal,
gills pulsing, silent in greyness,
sensing the thrashing flesh above.

Board riders windmill their arms
toward the bigger breakers
curling to push them shoreward.

The hunter below, his appetite
sated by an earlier meal,
holds his position, bored as a stump
with his anthropomorphic reputation
of deadly intent.

SORRENTO BEACH

She squirms deeper into the sand, mounds
it up to the towel's edge so grains
of sand can't cling to her wet skin,
needing warmth to keep the chill away.

Seawater drops skitter down over goose
flesh on her arms and legs. She stretches out
on another towel, grinds her body farther
into the sand, nestles in the hollow, basking.

Music strains through the air from a radio
on a nearby blanket. A tune, too soft
to be recognized, mixes with the swoosh
of pounding surf, drone of an airplane engine,
distant shriek of a child jumping into cold water.

Muted sound fills her head, stuffs her ears with
the cotton of noise. Languorous, surrounded
by people, she hears dim conversations that sound
like bees buzzing, hovering around her, protective,
even though oblivious to her presence.

Lulled by human voices, sheltered by anonymity,
she can listen, finds it possible to lie, unmoving, until
the breeze comes up again, cooled by the Pacific.
Never enough towels to cover her shivering body.

She remembers: summer was like that, seeking
warmth at the beach, returning home to her room
behind blinds that closed out the world.

SPRING FORWARD

so I reset hour hands slow ahead,
full stop the night before—
I'm no night owl—
wrap up cozy an hour early,
big mistake, the elusive Sandman
keeps his own hourglass. He and
Mama Nature see through this
mortal trick, shuffle off in long,
black gowns, just not in my
neighborhood. I toss the
fitful turns, flickeringly dream
of limp clocks, languid watches
a la Dalí (bet Salvador had this problem),
until wakey, wakey seven a.m.
looks like six; no chirping
birds, popping flowers,
breezy sunshine, still dark.
Is it spring yet?

SUMMER

comes soon,
loudly sing cuckoo, a serenade.
The sun stays up higher, longer,
lets me travel farther,
like brighter sunsets,
watch children jump into
the pool, splashing, racing.
I stay out later, still return
before nightfall, during
an extended twilight,
drive to where I drove
before, pushing
into later movies,
theater, dinners,
easier to overcome
my trepidations
of nighttime driving,
when lines seem oddly
skewed, a few more
shadows flicker,
unexpected,
familiar destinations
seen as strange.

THE COLLECTIVE

A catch in the throat at beauty as grey streaks
stream across a fiery setting. Crepuscular,
the light dims, but tomorrow the sun flares—
some will miss the renewal. Having worn

out their bodies, like coats, into ripped seams
and sagging pockets, they hung them up.
Their essence is webbed with strands
of individual life into the Collective

which absorbs, amoeba-like,
all shattered refugees of wars,
those destroyed by illness,
by stress of living. Held

until the shreds kept alive in the memory
of the last human friend wear away,
leaving ghosts in the mist,
distinct, but not earth-solid.

I sniff the other's unique smell, hear
words with special meanings, replay
tones, touches. Essence found, felt,
held, accessible when I need it.

THE FIRST DAY OF THE WAR

Forty-five years they have
played together
on instruments centuries old—
strings, precisely fashioned,
glow from tender care
and the best use of their magic.

Haydn, Beethoven, Bartok
would marvel
at the freshness
given to their compositions
by the musical skill
of this quartet.

These men breathe as one,
concentrate
on their music,
yet talk to each other
with an arch of an eyebrow,
a glance sideways,
a finger movement so fast
the audience is unaware.

The blanket of sound
covers us, soothes us,
a brief palliative
to the angst churned up
by the outside world.

THE OCTOPUS

is deadly to mollusks,
crustaceans, other
small creatures.

Imprisoned, the animal
reveals its fluidity, slithers
its tentacles, circles them,
pushes their saucer-like disks
to suck against the aquarium glass.

Colors change from tan
to orange to spotted brown
matching the shade of rocks
or a sand mantle. Lurking,
it darts out to poise
its beak, envelop captured
mussels, scallops, snails.

I watch these small deaths,
remote and detached,
safe and dry
outside the glass cell.

THE SUN, THE MOON

I can stare at the sun without
blinking, the smoke is so thick.
I watch it change from pumpkin
to vermilion through a thickening
pall of smoke dragged down
to the sea by Santa Ana winds.
The fire storm sucked up moisture
from trees, vacuumed out the air
from buildings. Everything
collapsed where it passed.

A young girl wearing gloves
sifts through ashes, broken
glass, looking for her diary.
A man weeps over lost photos,
the piano that held them a twisted
pile of strings. Neighbors
hold each other, for a while.

At sunset, the desolation
forms black holes ringed with
shooting flames sweeping over ridges.
The rising moon gives little light.
It's not a hearty harvest moon
but a sickle of rust, a pale
imitation of the burnt sienna sun.

As the fires die down and the smoke
clears, no one will be able to stare
directly at the sun. The moon
will show a little more of itself
each night as the rusty tinge fades.

THIS DAY NO LONGER MATTERS

Pain fires up into the orange
setting of the sun. Purpled
shadows crawl the room's
interior, cloud the light.
Dimmed eyes watch
the green of life,
the exterior world darkens.
Tormented breaths
whistle through the
oxygen, the tanks,
the plastic strings
of attachment
wound like nested snakes
holding captive,
still longer, one
who would be freed
to melt into the bleak
black lurking just
behind the orange.

NIGHT OWL

The owl, wings beating like strong fans
propelled in a down-pillowed silence,
one breath short of absolute quiet,
sails over the chaparral.

The round "ooh ooh" of its cry
nibbles at my dream self,
picking out the soft parts,
leaving the hard bits, like
candied cubes in a fruitcake.

My sleep has been too shallow to
cover my ears, so I wake to hard
thoughts and try to submerge
again deep enough to rest, to
resist the tension that binds my
shoulders, my neck, the alternating
hollow and platform of my spine.

Instead, I pretend that I am flying
with the owl, seeing through his eyes.
I see the mouse scurry under a
frayed leaf, just a shade too late.
I see the rabbit, ears twitching
with fear, paralyzed, betrayed
by the shining of its eyes.

I see my body open to the owl's
beak should it care to tear at it and
rip me open like Prometheus,
punished for daring to be human.

I am what I see.
The owl knows.
It does not want me.

THIS IS NOT A POEM

After Magritte

This is a thought about a poem.

A poem cannot write itself,
it must be thought of first.
If I create one, it will exist,
but a person with a similar thought
will write a different poem. For me
each word will have a specific meaning,
not the same for others.
I emphasize a certain alliteration,
another may allow an alternate one.
I punctuate for pauses I want, another
may pick a different point.
Stanza breaks, enjamb-
ment, line breaks, all mine.

If I change word order, the poem
is different, completely.
If I think of a poem one day, write
it two days later, it is different,
          I have already changed.
If I read these words aloud, not everyone
will hear them the same. Some may miss
a syllable or two, misunderstand my tone,
not recognize my pronunciation.
A poem, until it is written or spoken,
can only live inside the mind of the poet
who is the sole possessor of it.
Once written, the poem will still fluctuate,
shorten, lengthen, be edited, re-edited,
publication is not always final.

A poem in thought is a poem in waiting
I am thinking about writing a poem.

TIDEPOOL

Into the anemone's center,
into the fringed encirclement,
I push a finger, soft
explorer, held in delicate
though brief entrapment.

Blue-gray fronds wave
with the current as if
they were breathing.
Shells, seeming abandoned,
pick up hidden tiny legs,

kick up miniscule puffs
of sand. Surf grass spreads
green over wave-smoothed
stones, hides small snails
and owl limpets.

Their environment,
crushable, isolated, adding
zero gain to our national
wealth, leaks away through
rocky apertures, while
its treasury of stars
is plundered.

TOP OF THE HILL

Foxtails wave in the breeze,
wheatlike strands of thinning
hair on the crumbly dirt skull
of the hillside. I follow
the rocky trail as it
parts over a rise, turns,
zigzags toward the top.
I rest a moment, swallow
water, focus on shiny leaves
of live oak, red toyon berries.

Ahead, others kick up clods
of dirt as lug soles dig in. Quail
rousted from their roost
call *chicago*, *chicago* as they
polish the air with whirring wings.

I pretend I lead the few hikers
behind me, pretend I must eye their
progress as I stoop, pull foxtails from
my thick socks. As the grade steepens,
I move slower, time each step with a yoga

breath, visualize the familiar view from
the top of the hill. Lungs strain, I must halt,
wait for others to descend, reassure me
they have seen nothing new, nothing
more than what lives in my memory.

UNEXPECTED

A snow cover muffles
the sound of the river,
but it is there, ripping
out roots, hurling
them down into eddies
of churning pools.
Sheath ice glistens white,
shell-thin in unexpected
places. Crevices crack open.
Below the blue reflections
is the depth of blackness
where water rushes
over hard boulders.

I knew the ice could crack,
still it shocks.
The falling,
the eyes cast in desperation,
helpless, searching
for the one who can
rescue or turn back time.

The skin of the earth betrays me,
lets me walk on the ice
without thought,
lets me play on the surface,
then plunges me down, to
what-was-always-there.

UPROOTED

The tree stump's
truncated top,
below majesty,
below strength,
parallels
hard ground,

        its loss history:
leaves on windy
nights, their grip
released, propelled
somehow
to sail flyways.

Thin twigs
detached,
spun earthward.

Branches, lower,
       higher,
weighed in, bereft,
heavy enough to abandon
attachment, snapped off, left
pock marks on the trunk shaft.

Chemical warfare,
pitched-over wounds,
an attack circle
of advisors,
gardeners who resigned,
all prescribed
amputation and prayer.

The cutting stopped
at this stump,
table of cellulose, food
for worms and wishes.
I long to see shoots
and green babies.

Out of rich soil, root
tendrils poke upward.
Tentative, bony fingers
make skeletal gestures
skyward, beckon
branches, twigs, leaves
to return,
overcome separation,
begin regrowth,
give me back
the hollows,
the nests that filled them.

WAVES

The ocean washes my ankles,
chilling my reddened skin. Rocks
dent the soles of my feet, ripples
pull away effluvia, launch
small rivers, tumble stones into
metallic chatter. A rush
of foam and sandpipers dance
away with dainty ballet
steps. I try to follow them
to safety, but breaking waves
force me to stagger, dig my toes
deeper into silty pits. Undertow
tugs, tries to drag me to the deeps
where bones of poets who leapt
off ships or bridges marinate
in sand-filled eddies. I stand
in the shallows shaking, then
fall to my knees. The seventh
wave is not the last: they keep
coming, relentless, scrape
my body over pebbly ground.
I fight, reach dry sand,
stand exhausted but clear
of the waves,
free from danger,
of being overwhelmed
for a little while.

ALBINO CROW

I have never seen an albino crow.

Perhaps it is condemned
to death at birth,
to death by pecking,
to death by a hierarchy burdened
by a preordained authority.

"It is better not to see a white
reflection in the water where
a black reflection ought to be."

It is hard to fake blackness,
hard to hide a white head
under any color wing.

Perhaps there was one, once,
in fable or mythology, or in the
syllogistic list together with the
nonexistence of black swans,
or flightless birds, or
other facile, false beliefs.

If an albino crow exists,
survives the murderous nest,
the unforgiving nest,
the casting out,
it might live a squandered
life, wasted on apologies
because
it is not
black.

WHAT PRICE THIS PEARL?

My mind, like the ocean floor, is fertilized
by circling currents, streams that swirl
bits of thought until one embeds itself. Questions
irritate the web-like network of my mind.
A nucleus forms around the seed of sand,

displacing nothing, expanding by sharing
other people's lives, deaths, laughter.
I nurture the core, wait for the nucleus
to round to perfection, ready to be shucked
from the shell, the oyster of my brain.

It's plain.
Each of my children already has a pearl,
startling in its differences,
familial in its similarities.

WHEN MY HANDS WERE FULL

When my hands were full, I carried stones
in my mouth, dropped them at your doorstep.
Take these to build your walls, I said.

When my hands were full, I carried food
in my mouth, dropped it in your hand.
Feed your children, I said.

When my hands were full, I carried water
in my mouth, filled your bucket.
Water your crops, I said.

When my hands were full, I carried bullets
in my mouth, spat them beside your rifle.
Use these, I said, when there is no water,
there is no food, and your walls
cannot protect you.

HISTORY LIES BEYOND THE MILKY WAY

We peer into our past,
astronomers say,
into light emanations eons old,
before Neanderthals, before rulers
who taught us murder, wars
of subjugation, slavery,

who want us to feel miniscule—
commas in history's latest paragraph,
pests, infestations to be obliterated
without compunction, only saved,
sans heroics, to protect
our savior's reputations.

They err, we die.
We suffer, they turn away,
claiming our future must reflect our past.

The universe inside me;
is inside you.
Now is our space, our time and place.
We struggle to gather heart
and brain for energy and thought
within the perceived limits of reality.

Devotion to present living,
to projected plans, turns
the past to mere sufficiency
and not essential.
The past lies beyond the Milky Way."

V
In the Hands of
Oceanic Gods
Myth & Might

BEGINNING

God the mother, or godmother, or mother of god presents
        the loveable lizard

wobbly   bald   greedy
sucking with a frantic urgency,
pulling nourishment from its deep
birthplace inside the body, a fountain
that gushes forth with warmth, comfort, love.

A squeeze starts the lactation process, the instinctual
turning toward the breast takes over. It's amazing
the strength of the single-minded drive
for food, shelter, protection from the elements,
an ability to be a person
with pride, confidence, security.

This is the right of all humanity,
not a privilege, a right
for men, women, children.
What a wonder it is to create another life.

In the hospital delivery room, lights glaring
into my eyes, they placed him on my stomach,
his littleness frightened me,
but I looked at him and fell in love.

MAN'S WORK IS NEVER DONE

Their jaws are hinged with muscles
of such power that when those teeth close
and clamp down, the human flesh
is mutilated, torn, left bleeding.
In pre-history, before men tamed and taught them,
they would only have attacked for food
to fill their bellies
or nourish their pups.
Now they hunt on call for men,
hunt other men,
bottom-of-the-heap men
or women, children, anyone found in the wrong place
at an unfavorable time,
in questionable circumstance.
Better a bite than a bullet,
they say, not asking if brutality is requisite.
It's only suspicious citizens of lower class,
of criminal appearance,
guilty physiognomy,
dirty clothes.

The dog makes his decisions.
Wise canine nose smells out the guilt.
Clever canine brain sifts evidence,
weighs motive,
ponders rules of law,
and snaps his powerful jaw
onto the offending arm or leg.
He won't release unless he's told,
so there's no rush.
A smallish loss of blood,
torn flesh can always be sewn up,
not much the worse,
and even livid scars, though permanent,
eventually will fade.
If he's in pain,

well, he was ill-advised to be out here;
the color of his skin's no camouflage.

The leash is an extension of an arm
whose muscles yearn to switch to club
or pistol butt,
whose fingers clench
in memory of solid rounds of wood or steel,
whose palm remembers the reverberation
from the strength of blows
that once delivered, sprang back in recoil.
The warmth of all that feeling
still remembered rushes back into his body,
straightens up his spine.
He stands erect now, tall,
the smile wrinkles deepening around his eyes,
although his mouth stays grim,
and he watches,
stands and watches,
counts and watches, while
he drops the leash.

MOZART

White notes dance among folds in the
dark curtains draped inside his head:
semi-quavers, quarters, halves, wholes,
trills, grace notes and codas. Codas.

Flashing notes that he must seize, yes,
before they vanish, seize with care
like humming birds that labor to
breathe, so their thrumming hearts
pulse, empower his fingers to write.

His quick quill pens the notes, singed
black now by a fever to complete the
passage, end the clamor in his brain.

His candle, to give sufficient brilliance,
burns at both its ends. Sunlight—time
restrained, falls short. Night thrusts
sleep into struggle. The double-headed
glow burns out his natural allotment.
The fueling furnace cannot be stoked
fast enough. Two lifetimes must fuse
into one with his descendants caught
as ghosts between the two.

He, like any one of us, cannot foresee his
miserable end or know how it will flare
up, giving him, his music, incandescence
to illuminate the world for all of those
who call him Master.

THE BIG PICTURE

Where did we come
from? What are we?
Where are we going?

Gauguin painted
these words on his
big picture, created
figures in shades
of gold and brass,
creatures beyond
nature or their island
world, floated them
from birth, through
Eden, toward idols
rising from the
underground. Place
his words, their meaning,
on a balance scale:

all of mankind
on one side,
the artist's giant ego
on the other.

CHOICES

Fat dove
crunching along the bricks,
paralyzed by the permutation of possibilities,
stills,
awaits choices.

By a lantern light reflected from tent cloth,
boundaries become visible.
Wings batter the envelope,
claws scrabble over clay,
Mythical Roc,
bigger than life.

Burned-out cats snuff rat trails,
amazing on the mountain side.
Something swims in the soup.
Quick!
Pull it out before it drowns,
fire all the questions,
shoot out the answers; oracle
salutes into the void, miracle
farts into the night,
belches of laughter,
silhouettes of needles
too weak to stand alone
must quiver thorns
into a melting halo.

Pump it up
higher,
higher,
leap into space,
sore knees on landing,
THAT is for sure.

ODYSSEY

Frog eggs and mold,
mouse cells and yeast
cushioned in a nest of mucous,
slippery with slime,
flow into weightlessness.

Steel mutes the atmospheric rush
guarding the aluminum womb
cloistered in a cylinder clattering into orbit.
The yoke of gravity monitors direction.
Probes' tick-off-making, dandruff flakes
that snow into ridged containers
touched by gentian stains of microscopic
viewing when the photographic plates are primed.

Frog mother, lagging back on earth,
flicks a forked tongue, fastens onto someone else's child,
gulping wings and body,
so fulfilling nature's ordinance.
Mouse father snipping bits of grass
hordes seeds and leaves, a hedge
against the winter's deprivation.
Frog and mouse have paid in full for knowledge:
now they must receive some validation
for their chilling sacrifices.

ABOUT DRAGONS

Each tooth of a dragon
flung to the ground
by a president or
prime minister springs up
as a patriot ready with
aimed Kalashnikov.

Men seek the dragon
secluded in his cave,
steal his precious gold
scales, reverse alchemy,
transmute them
into tanks or mortars.

His fire flamed out,
the dragon is left
in the dark, alone,
scales ripped off,
children torn to bits.

A toothless, naked,
wrinkled lizard,
no longer able
to create troops
or offer gold,
he embodies still
the power of myth
to foster reason
in some human minds.

ABOUT VEILS

Gauze veils taunt, quiet
the broadcast voice;
seekers uncover
mutilation, a monster,
numinous Venus
draped and balanced
on her Botticelli shell.

Veils titillate,
as, one by one,
each falls away
and naked Salome
dances to cause
an enemy's death.

Veils accessorize,
obfuscate
cached truths. Veils
must be ripped apart
to let the flame
of disclosure blister
the torn edges,
to let fire balls
ignite and light
the exit route,
let truth escape
the woven
cover of lies.

ABRAHAM'S CHOICE

Bedouins wander with black tents and flocks of sheep,
temporary landlords in the shadows of the golden walls.
Inside Jerusalem, people flow between the quarters.
Each group asserts its claim to sovereignty,
defends its separate enclave from the rest.

Mohammed sprang up to Allah from the rock beneath the dome.
Under the rock, in the Western Wall,
written prayers to Yahweh fill the cracks between the stones.

From a balcony, I see the Via Dolorosa, where processions
wind along the streets on Christian holy days.
Copts, Armenians, Ethiopians, Greeks, monks, priests
raise up icons, clench fabled relics of a favored saint.

I see beyond the walls where an ancient people,
returned to Zion from diaspora, reclaimed the desert,
planted olives, cured them in oils and spices,
planted grapes, made wine.

Then, they built out farther, past Masada,
broiling in the summer sun, where a Roman army
camped below failed to starve resistors out,
past Megiddo, site of excavations that tell the history of centuries.
The tribes that shared this place so long ago still do.
Armageddon has not happened, but the wounds made
by religion suppurate in Israel, Jerusalem, and far beyond.

The devil dines on narrow minds, his cutlery
a battery of rocks and bottles, rubber bullets,
bombs secreted in the trunks of cars,
no outrage terrible enough to satiate his hunger.

Father Abraham, the patriarch
of Jew and Muslim both,
may have to choose between his children.

BANNERS

I followed the litany as directed:
>spelled my name so the guard could match it to the list,
>parked in the designated place,
>turned right, then left, looking for the specified banner,
>a pink and green tulip in a purple vase, hung from a polished
>mahogany dowel, gold finials on the ends.

Each house is pale: yellow, blue, green, nothing vivid here.
Each house is fronted by a xerophytic display: one nopal,
>one ocotillo, a small patch of crushed gravel, and
>a flagstone path leading from the sidewalk to the patio.
Each house has a tile roof of dull Spanish red.
Each house's front door faces in a different direction from its neighbor.

There are no people on the street, no SUVs, no skateboards, no bicycles.

There are many banners:
>elephants and a few donkeys
>hearts, shamrocks, turkeys
>pines, cedars, lilies
>Martha Stewart quilts
>poodles, pooches, and cats
>golf clubs, golf balls, and tees

I sense the ghosts of banners that will never be here:
>no Kwaanza, no Martin Luther King
>no Quince de Septiembre, no Cesar Chavez
>no Chanukah menorahs, no six-pointed stars
>no chopsticks, no fans, no good luck kanjis
>no nursery rhymes, no Mother Goose, no Peter Pan
>no pairs of women, no pinups
>no Che, no Fidel, no Mao, and

nothing at all that bears a coiled snake and the words: "Don't tread
on me."

283

BECOMING A DRAGON

In the desert, among bare skull-shaped
rocks, a lizard scuttles to a tiny cave.
Quick. I seize his tail. He wriggles
free, the tail left twisting in my palm.
I close my hand, feel my lizardness.

Wrinkled loose skin, drab-colored,
a loner, mind not on females,
he sees his future as reality—
        becoming a dragon
        blowing fire storms
        armored with scales
                like the big boys—
        famous fearful beasts
        thundering through skies
        burning villages
        wasting people
        devastating land. Powerful.

Goggle-eyed, the lizard slithers
his day away, gobbling stray flies,
munching, in his mind,
gizzard of the golden goose,
lion heart of Richard,
delicacies reserved to dragons.

He has faith.
The myth is that dragons are mythical.

COMIX I

In synthetic uniforms tight as a second
skin, streamlined bodies fly,
mount cycles, crouch in open cars,
summoned by enforcers unable to purge
crime lords from grubby precincts.
Cartoon heroes drag aging victims
out of burning structures, save
the weak, the fearful, the children.

Pow-Smash-Crash

Villains are thrashed, weapons smashed,
rockets lose their red glare as terrorists,
now bearded and turbaned
instead of uniformed and helmeted,
are savaged. The world changes,
comic heroes don't. With muscles,
sheer strength, all will be fixed.

Pow-Smash-Crash

COMIX II

Along the canyon of the boulevard,
where sidewalks edge the asphalt,
hooligans threaten women, children.

The breast-bulging, second sex
comic book heroine strides, leaps,
challenges criminals,
bats bullets back to the perps,
all unarrestable under ordinary rules.

She bears the unbearable
burden of innocents attacked.

Worker, protector,
determiner, provider,
Wonder Woman,
Supermom,

save us.
Save us all.

COMIX III

The gross-featured short ones,
mischief-riddled katzenjammers
have goals, yes, that's true,
to pick off cherries, pineapple
bits from an upside-down cake,
grab a pie from the kitchen
window sill where it cools.

Mama yells, waves her
rolling pin. Wobbling
on her fat legs, top knot
shaking, she chases
the little ragamuffins
who run with their loot,
fall on sugar-smeared
faces and can still
go home again, having
never cut any ties.
Mama, forever
forgiving mama,
will always be waiting.

SIRENS

Sleepless, ears alert for klaxons,
alarming signals—troubles for
someone—ambulance awaited,
heart in mouth, and
with luck a companion, reassurer,
hand holder, entrance handler,
information giver;

timing essential, paramedics
required, someone has fallen,
wheelchair-bound or floor-
bound—a pick-up of sorts.

Red lights flash with sirens
of death, as Ulysses told his
seamen, so they plugged
their ears against the song
of the Sirens, but curiosity
overcame caution so he
(tied to the mast) listened,
unable to follow the
hypnotic sound.

Ulysses was a risk-taker,
and this is not mythology.

DROWNING

Blind feet seek chunky pebbles and
curb-cliffs that hover over asphalt.
Gaping, it gulps flounderer
with flailing arms,
up to the "o"
like a Munch mouth,
black-rimmed,
frozen oral cavern,
the secret lair of stalagmites.
"The better to swallow you, my dear."

Bubbles are touching harsh reeds.
Hippo nostrils rise,
betraying horned nails
that mud-wallow
and pound the ancient ooze into
the bones of archaeopteryx.
Webbed wings soared and bore
death into the sodden ferns
while the earth bled into the stones.

Miles into the time zone,
still there was no dog with two heads,
no god giggling over the entrails of a kid,
no watching over the ramparts,
altar balls, or curved horns.

Waved off in landing on the crest,
rudder down,
masts smashed,
canvas ripped,
let it fly.

STRONG WOMEN

Greeks saw Amazons as heroic women,
daughters of the sword/shield,
battlefield slaughterers of men
who fell before slings, maces.
Men insured continuation of
the race, freed femmes to fight
state enemies and crooks.

Wonder Woman used a gold
lasso, forced truth from power
brokers, tossed bad guys out
of windows, sent hog-tied
rats, in stripes, to jail.

Disguised with glasses,
ordinary clothes, when stripped
for action, she wore a red bustier,
starred/striped, a gold tiara.

Myth:
>   Her origin a mist-obscured
>   island in an unknown sea
>   where all were Amazons.
Reality:
>   A few strong women, just
>   a few, move up corporate levels,
>   even in the start-up valley,
>   silicon still an ingredient,
>   the glass ceiling stands.

The fight goes on.

TEA PARTY

One soldier guest blows in
from a humvee, dragging
his tangled limbs.
One marine guest, blasted
off a dock, emerges
charred to cinder black.
Citizens wonder if such
men conquer, ponder
glasses, helmets,
disguises that fool the gullible.

All guests ascend the staircase
where white wings unfold
above tea and manna
spread on shining leaves.
All guests mourn the wounds
that dot white tablecloths
with crimson berries.
They shoulder double barrels
of frustration, ignorance;
wipe their rumps with their
return tickets and are afraid
to look over their shoulders,
afraid to look ahead.

DOLPHINS

ride the bow waves of boats.
Poseidon's pets
cannon through the water like torpedoes
out to sink a school of anchovies,
sardines, or any small flashy fish.
From the shallows I watch a
dolphin ride the curl of the waves,
see a long shape glide in and out,
shed drops of water that reflect
as a silver chain connected to
the gleeful shadow as it
leaps through the water.

Myths claim dolphins are rescuers
of little boys, men on paddle boards
attacked by sharks, even the poet,
Arion, abandoned at sea in
ancient times.

Where are the stories of these
bottle-nosed mammals saving
girls, rescuing women from
"worse than death"—those few
who flung themselves from pirate
or slaving vessels—clung to life
savers overboard during a wild
yacht party, or those with seaman's
papers, sailing their own boat
when weather shifted radically
and without warning, casting
them adrift, endangered?

FIG THEORY

One bite through edible black
skin exposes the tiny
flesh-colored tongues, wiggling,
inviting each small bite,
palate pleasing, sliding easily
down the throat, calming
fire in the blood.
A fruit to be consumed
slowly, luxuriously, together
with another mouth,
bit by bit, not guzzled,
not raped, but enjoyed
in dalliance and delight.

Eve's first mistake was to use
only the leaf of the fig tree.
Had she chosen wisely,
enjoyed a fig with Adam,
instead of an apple,
she might have led him gently
out of Eden as his equal
in life to look for another
beautiful garden, not another
country to conquer,
not other humans
to humble in atonement
for the sin of understanding.

GARUDA

Mythic, eagle-like

    as Lord Vishnu's mount blocks out

        the sun, wreaks havoc.

CONTEST OF THE GODS

Fire ash combines with yellow powder to dot the foreheads of every
    Hindu here.
Smoke drifts into our eyes, makes them tear.
I sniff the remembered smells of India: scented oil, sweat, burning wood.

The marble floors are dulled by dirt tracked in on jelly shoes, thongs,
            calloused bare feet.
Even so, the devout prostrate themselves. When they rise, their saris and
            respectful trousers seem unstained.

Nearby, small fires melt butter into oleaginous mounds that ease into
            putridity.
Worshippers make balls of the butter, hurl them at the shapeless bulk
            behind the enclosure.

There is enough light from the smoking candles to illuminate the target
            but not enough to reveal gaps where a face is missing.

Kali, the tall mound represents Kali, wreathed in white flowers as a
    goddess should be,
            even one being defiled.
The butter balls are meant to punish her, to make her pay for
    daring to challenge Siva
            in the contest for best dancer among the gods.

Kali lost when Siva removed his leg and threw it toward the
    heavens, but she dishonored
            her consort, and her punishment might please him.

Myth is immutable, maybe so is daily life, yet we ask for Siva's help.
        The Destroyer can also be a savior.
        Siva, from the darkness of his shrine,
        will hear us,
        will help us.

IN MY VIEW

from my hidden interior perch,
Escher-like railing strut
marches toward a vanishing point.
Hanging lamps throw shadows
form grids where corners
meet at right angles.
Roofs on upper floors slant,
supported by pillars. A distant
stairway runs down to lower levels.

My companion, a radio, breaks
into forties music; lyrics sing
of cornfields, sunshine, when
today into tomorrow mattered,
peace was real, at least for us,
and we cared for each other.

Midas is king, acquisition trumps
morality. If others can't make it,
let them perish. Here, on this
weekday night, nothing
moves, residents,
consciences clear, sleep.
They do not see me in their dreams.

OH, FOR TRUE TRAGEDY

for Hector, mutilated, tied by
Achilles behind his chariot, dragged
three times around Troy
under Apollo's approving eye.
Kings took the field, proud to kill,
to die, corpses mourned by all,
consigned to fire. Their children,

warrior princes, first in harm's way,
led troops, loyal even
when their cause was unclear—
fruitless occupation of a hostile land,
a ruler seeking reputation,
or a god, offended, whispering
in a human ear, urging vengeance.

Zeus weighed men's lives
on his balance scale, eliminated
lightweights with a thunderbolt,
permitted heavyweights,
if they sacrificed to him,
to be granted riches,
not on Olympus,
but in an earthly dynasty.

WHOM THE GODS WOULD DESTROY

they first make mad.
—Euripides

Apollo wrenches his chariot up—gods
are above gravity. Horses pull with mighty
muscles, pure energy. Hooves thrash upwards.
Earth is lit. Sun power. If you ride
with Apollo, you will never see night.

Boundaries on the planet's skin
      meaningless,
color of people's skin
      meaningless.
Olympians demanded blood

sacrifice; we kowtow, genuflect,
prostrate ourselves. Pray
for consolation, a lover, a job, health.
No response. Clerics threaten
Armageddon—date certain. The date

passes. They change the date.
Worshippers of one chosen deity
fear, distrust deities of others. Holocausts
come. Earthquakes, tsunamis, tornados,
wildfires, floods, volcanic eruptions.

People light candles, burn incense,
dance with fury, bang drums.
Each person bleats to a chosen god whose
evil punishment shocks them, believes—
expects—this time, God will intervene.

RASHID AL-DIN

eager to serve the khan, gathered
the chronicles of heralded leaders
and wrote Ghazan's compendium—
the history of the Mongols
and the culture of the world.

Moses, Muhammad, Jesus,
Siddhartha, even Alexander
speak to us in Arabic or Persian,
appear in swirling illustrations
that cover museum walls,
proclaim the legacy of Genghis.

Rashid's family, steeped
in Judaism, denied apostasy.
There was no rending of clothes,
no cursing of his name.
They welcomed the honors
bestowed by the court.

Rashid, touted as a convert,
might have found his way,
a meager price to pay
for glory in this world—
believed the deal sealed,
the toleration of his Jewish faith.

With jealous words, his enemies,
original powers in the Mongol
court, plotted his demise,
paraded his head and his son's
throughout the city,
freely proclaimed the death
of the "infidel Jew."

RIDING A CAROUSEL HORSE

The center pillar, mirrored,
throws rainbows
over circling horses glistening
with layers of enamel
over hard, carved wood.

The gulping music sounds
like a circus calliope,
but there are no clowns here.
Brave children ride stallions
whose open mouths, bared teeth
discourage kisses.

Scaredy-cats cower
on stationary mounts,
no chance to snatch a gold ring.
The operator weaves
between beasts, plucks
red paper tickets from small hands,

smiles slyly, swings to the music,
dances backwards. The child,
proud of his daring, sees familiar
faces blur as he whirls away,
searching for a special person

seen, only to disappear
until his rising, falling horse
returns him safe, not abandoned,
not stranded next to a silent
carousel that he can't ride
back without a gold ring
or a silver coin.

THE MOON

in full phase spins
its cycloid curve
through top branches
of a white pine, dodges
arêtes of high peaks.

Moon watchers gave her
a goddess' name, Selene,
knowing only a woman
could exist for eons
as a reflection of the male,
Helios, charioteer of the sun.

For eons she has rolled along
the ecliptic plane, not quite
faithful to the prescribed
course, for trillions
of human lifetime spans.

In bright day, the hypnotic
lure of Helios' sun blinds
unprotected gazers,
burns their skin. Selene
is visible only as a
delicate, papery disc.

Night, her time,
her incandescence
half-veiled in ragged
clouds, casts deep,
treacherous shadows,
misleads women
who wander the dark
into dangerous choices
from obscured vision
or too swift a move.

THE OUTBACK

Vastness. Hectares measure a station.
Red dirt rushes into red dirt, past desert
oak, gum trees. Others sleep close
to the slow-dying fire. I move away, watch
the firmament, astonishing arch above me.

Black holes, secret between sun systems
of captive planets, swirling nebulae in fanciful
configurations named by eye-weary
earthbound gazers. Comets whip through,
tails trailing, constellations named

for mythical creatures, like Python Woman
who carried her eggs in her mouth to Uluru, hid
them in a chasm, killed one enemy, one threat,
leaving the aboriginals—real originals—to retell
tales, use constellations, sky rotations,

guide the clans, plant, harvest, move across
the land, under starlight, dead white with
greenish tinge, enough to outline sharp rocks,
broken trees. Run from a real or imagined
enemy threat. No time to wait for sunrise.

I see the same starlight, waxy, cooler
than firelight, sense the weight, multitudes
of universes, earth horizons, black waves
melting into unseen distances. Isolated,
I shiver in my sleeping bag, inside

the heavy canvas swag, cold, hearing muffled
cries of unknown creatures, night hunters,
prey, sounds that seem to creep closer until
dawn, at last, people stir, call out, claiming
a good sleep, relieved to see others, daylight.

WHERE WAS GOD?

god came to her and demanded the keys
to her car, her old beat-up, scratched and
faded pickup. He claimed it was a fair tithe.
"Why should you possess when I do not?
Why must I beg for what should be a gift?"

god said. He came to her hidden in the
body of a young deep-breathing man with
a harsh voice, a hard hand, and no caring
at all for her feelings and her fears.

The car, transmuted, became a part of her
definition of herself, her ego, her goals
and her gains. All hers! Anger oiled her
hesitation. Belief denied that god would
violate humanity, steal dignity,
demand possession. god's insistence

hardened her. Resentment rose up, settled
into her throat, puckered up her lips and
sent spit right into god's assumed visage
of a common man whose stubbled chin had
unwiped sweat and snot dribbling over it.

"It's only a car, a cultural icon, a monetary
shibboleth, worth no more than a farthing,
no more than a sou," people said. She agreed,
knew the smart, sensible way, but when it

broke upon her consciousness that this
was not god at all but a sniveling crook,
a thief, a gonif (in her family's lexicon),
all the smarts fled, and all the indignation
stood up and was counted.

"Why . . . ?"   "What did . . . ?"   "What was . . . ?"

all the queries were asked when no one
who could have answered them was alive.
Wisdom, loose in the mouths of the
questioners, assumed that she had been
given no choice, had been executed
without appeal, without recourse.

She might have hoped to escape,
gambling that he could not
commit murder. Bystanders
heard the shots come fast, little
time to be aware, feel the pain
of tearing, know that life was gone.

Her brain was blown out, the unique
self-obliterated. Her arms waved
and jerked as she crashed down.
When the blood dried, her hair
was stuck to the asphalt.

Sirens howled. Radios flashed
information: license number,
color, model, direction. The car
was flushed out and chased, and
chased some more. Bullets
formed a rain of retribution.

HIJACKED PICKUP CRASHES. SUSPECT KILLED.

And where was god?
god had been there. he had
demanded a small sacrifice, a tithe,
from a believer who had denied
him, so god took by force the greatest
sacrifice and claimed it as fair and
just, a tribute to his power.

THE SHOEMAKER'S SON

Wing, 9 ½ EEE shuffled along.
Tongue-tied, broken in, he often
held his tongue. Quiet suited him
until he found his sole mate,

a well-heeled rubber magnate,
Buck, who was straight-laced
but highly polished, kept instep
with the latest in leather.

Having pulled himself
up by his bootstraps,
Buck was not a loafer, went
to oxford, shoe-horned

his way into the high top
of industry. Buck and Wing
walked together, one was right,
the other left. They never had a spat.

Buck and Wing, both male,
could not legally be paired
here, so they traveled abroad,
shared a bag, learned to clog

from a vamp with a brogue,
sported with a friend, Spike,
got a lift out of their insoles,
got a boot out of life.

LOST BOY

Did you think you could fly? Leaping
off the 10th floor, gravity's pawn,
dying in the post-game afternoon,
a flailing figure watched in horror?

Why? The conjectures begin:

    Schoolmates with pills, challenging,
    daring you, take one. Your mind is locked?
    Well, here is the key, and the world swirls a cape
    around you, revs up superpowers.

        You thought: I can do what no one else
        can, I can do what no one can.

    Taunts, because you had a "special friend."
    The jocks teased, sneered at your denials. Prove
    masculinity? How? Easier to retreat
    from being outed, pain of unlikeness,
    fly away forever. Be with Pan's boys.
    All lost, all immortal.

        It will be forgotten.
        The bad will be forgotten.

    Sudden blackbirds beat strong wings
    inside your head, pull a black veil,
    blot out sunlight. A flock from the depths,
    their beaks tear at your brain, your eyes. A terror
    you never felt before steals your breath,
    forces escape into space, free to fall.

        You left a hole in the world.
        The secrets you took with you
        will always be secrets.

VI
Ordinary and Luminous
In Praise of Objects

EYES

See the rafter high above?
It is surfaced with an ever-changing eye.

A sloe-eyed Egyptian hieroglyph,
its faint outline is darkened by kohl.

Mongolian, with an epicanthic fold, graceful
and narrow, it slants upward.

Round and vapid, animation eye, cartoon-like;
it is wide in its innocence.

Wandering, strabismic, it gazes toward the
inner side, the disconcerting eye.

The aging, cataract eye, filmy, peering,
weeping, oozes, loses its vitreous humor slowly.

It is the third eye.
It is the all-seeing eye.
It is the blind eye.
It is not an eye at all.

It is watching me.

FASTENINGS

I sell the laces that hold together
bits of leather cut and shaped to
a specific mold. I do not sell
the shoe.

I sell the string that secures a
balloon, helium-filled and tugging
against a small-fisted child's grasp.
I do not sell balloons.

I sell the buttons that close the shirt
front, holding it taut over shoulders
and across the chest. The shirt must
be bought somewhere else.

I have thread and needles,
zippers, snaps, hooks and eyes.
I can handle buckles, cords
and grommets for a belt, but
whole constructions are
beyond my powers.

Do not expect that I can offer
more than bits and pieces.
A whole, a finished product,
is beyond my power.

WHITE PICKETS

Unlatched,
hinged slats
swing back,
clatter board against board,
whine with the wind,
smack dying dandelions,
lanky in the unkempt yard,
puff-headed until seeds wing
onto the deserted porch
next door, next door to that.

One lone window
stares toward
the horizon
beyond prairies
of flattened bunkers.

FLASHLIGHT

I twist my wrist and the light scatters
away from me, sends my demons
skittering into the corners, unseen.
The beam swings earthward

where broken pavement trips my feet.
My mind is addled by the transition
from darkness to illumination.
If challenges goad us to enlightenment,

my darkness is full of them. I hold
the source of light in my hand.
My thumb controls its power. I fear
the singularity of choices I must make—

tranquilize my angst or face it,
turn away from a burnt-out friend
or listen, learn to understand him;
trust an adult child, cut him loose

to soar or crash as I watch.
The flashlight beam is finite. Within
its circle of light I have to isolate,
choose my one clear path.

CAR CEMETERY

Helter-skelter, the frames
pile up, exposed, as are the
corpses on the Tower of
Silence waiting for vultures
to clean off their bones.

Steel bodies lie torn open
to expose internal parts.

Paint peels off like
flayed skin. With a flash
of flat color or metallic glisten,
the streaks stretch long,
edged by brown rust.

Windshields were crazed,
then they cracked, vomited
glass across hoods, over fenders.

The tight circle of a steering
wheel was shattered into uneven
arcs around a spear-like shaft.

Slashed and burned torsos of
upholstered seats lie scattered.

Scavengers stripped the chassis,
plucked out the useful chunks,
and left the skeletons of Chevys,
Hondas, even limousines
(no longer arrogant).

A man stalks the lanes between
these ruptured frames, searching
for the one that was a coffin for a
lover buried in a different place.

She flew, all four wheels off
the ground, spinning and smashing
when the tires blew out on impact.

She crashed all alone into concrete,
innocent, ignorant, until her mind
surrendered to a red tide.

He seeks the place where, shocked
into a shriek, she may have yelled
a word, granting reason to
senselessness, a message to
assuage his need to understand.

An echo is all he seeks.

There is nothing here but
mute remains awaiting
resurrection.

They will be born again,
into new bodies.
Their chrome will smile,
offering to the world
a wide and shining rictus.

HI-TECH

A grandfather clock with pendulum beard
counterweighted, wheels within wheels,
chimes that sometimes gave the air
a headache—bonged into the next room.

Black Forest cuckoo popping in and out,
a Swiss miss pirouetting in a dirndl skirt,
amusing to watch, and musical,
if only you remembered to rewind.

I had a clock that was unique;
its hands stood still, the face revolved.
Others had several faces, counting
seconds or even phases of the moon.

Now, my clock is digital,
electrical (with back-up battery),
it gives me big red numbers
and a flashing colon.

TRAVELLING LIGHT

The suitcase holds my outer layer,
clothes swathed mummy-like in plastic
bags, all folded and tucked in:
an airy blouse for summery days,
a sweater, just in case.
I add a dressy skirt I hope I need to wear,
and stockings, flat in cellophane, that
look like skin without the flesh.

I have all the room I need, now.
Lacy panties occupy the space once
filled by boxer shorts. There are bras
instead of cotton undershirts, and
a nightgown, not so new but never worn.
Since there is no razor case, my makeup
kit expands and spreads out,
nestling into any sheltering spot
that it can find.
I have all the room I need.

DOLLS

We stood our dolls in rows,
counted individuals,
claimed ownership.
One of mine had stiff,
corn-yellow braids, a
too-starched pinafore.
One of yours, a Cinderella
of a contrary Bo-Peep, was
fastened to a limp-tailed lamb.
Ours, a red-clad soldier, had
a phony leather Sam-Browne belt,
the only male.

A German song of dolls our
English grandma crooned.
She rocked and cuddled us,
gave us the tenderness our
mother never understood.

We loved the dolls, so we
expected them to make us worthy,
teach us to be women, but their
waxy lips clamped closed, their
long-lashed eyelids, opened, shut,
mechanical and flat,
with each new pose.

I abandoned them, grew up,
gave all my dolls to you and
brought you more as
travel souvenirs. New
collectibles, I thought, but
you felt malice in my gifts.

I look beyond the faded clothes,
the brittle hair and

cracked doll cheeks.
I see the dolls as memories.
You see them as antiques
you own and smile at
their monetary worth.

FINGERS

I have ten fingers, ten, to open, close,
oppose, clench nails into angry crescents,
then arch to approximate the reverse
Balinese curve. Ten, dainty and poised,
trill on a keyboard, musical or otherwise.
I need all to countdown to a knockout.

I have nine fingers, nine. One tried to
stop the backlash of a thrashing rope.
It failed. I mourned it, dreamt of a
replica, a wraith to fill the aching
hollow where the real one used to be.
Fewer planets, now, are counted one by one.

I have eight fingers, eight. Wrenched from
a trap that, baited for bear, caught instead
a gold-starved nugget seeker. The thumb
was abandoned to save the hand, a sacrifice
of one apostle to save the others. Bagged and sewn
by a specialist, this trophy will not decorate a wall.

I have seven fingers, seven. The snake that
buried its fangs, shot the poison into my
circulating blood, and died with a rattle of
death as it wrapped around my wrist,
a flaccid tourniquet. One less day of the
week to count, my weeping is diminished.

I have six fingers, six. Cancer from neglected
cysts, penetrated nearly to the bone and,
unless excised, would have eaten all.
Now each joint counts itself among the
fortunate. 666 is the sign of Satan's curse.
Wallow in that or cherish the survivors.

I have five fingers, five. These no longer

remember their fellows, the touching of each
point of a pentagram. The accident that killed
the driver, split my finger on a windshield
shard. Mourning my friend, shrouded for a
while the loss I had to bear yet one more time.

I have four fingers, four. With the crab-like
grasp I did not want to execute, I tried to
save my wedding ring. It fell into a creek
where thermal jets propelled their fetid vapors
upward, caught my finger in a boiling spout,
left one season less of separation, singlehood.

I have three fingers, three. One is a thumb
so I can still oppose if I create the chance.
Nourishment is more a challenge than a need.
Regrets and memories of what I once
possessed fill my mouth with ashes. One of
the genii's wishes is gone, my losses stay.

I have two fingers, two. Clumsy in my effort
to exercise and raise my spirits, I tried to
balance, gripless, on a stationary bike and
tumbled off. My finger, sticking out, was
captured in a wheel of flashing struts.
I choose either "up" or "down," not both.

One finger, one I have. One to stir the pot,
to lick and feel the breeze, to poke a hole
through a leaf, to point the way, to raise
up high in order to bring notice to myself.
One, visible image of those that vanished,
compels me to chew it off, like a mad artist.

No fingers. I have no fingers. My ruined
hands look like those of a leper, destroyed
by putrefaction and decay. I touch with my
elbows, the sides of my hands. It is not
enough. I have four full senses, but the world
will never be the same as it was when I had five.

FEBRUARY THE FIFTEENTH

Chocolate scrapes on the edges of ribbed
bonbon papers, crust like blood dried
around a wound, or dropped from fingers
stabbed by thorns on the long stems of roses.
Red roses, expensive flowers, that falsely
promised lovely odors, full blooms, instead
exuded the early sweetness of vegetation soon to rot.
The buds drooped with black-tinged lips still
tightly closed as they followed empty boxes
into trash cans, onto rubbish heaps.

Open, heart-shaped boxes let their emptiness
apologize. They misled us so when they conspired
with the trite and pretty, pink and silver, glitter
of the cards. They made us think they really
promised love with their plush-puffed tops and
silk-striped ribbons. Tawdry in plain daylight, they
burn like any ordinary cardboard would.

The flames create charred fingers that curl and
move as though they were alive, beckoning us
to come closer. Our eyes smart and our brows sweat.
The water that falls on the flames is salty.

Here, we pay homage to the son of Venus.
This is his funeral pyre. He was condemned
to death because he lied to us.

POOR FISH

A lead weight zings through air,
catapults through water, buries
itself in bottom weeds. Hidden,
it teases out tendrils bearing gifts:
a cluster of salmon eggs, oozing
red dye and a fish smell;
a globe of chartreuse dough
that wafts an odor and beckons
with mica-flecked curls.
A metal lure wiggles downward
then flashes backward, offering
a deceptive, cannibal feast.
A bubble, floating on the surface,
trails a misshapen worm.

These hoaxes, these gilded baits,
swirl through the water.
Virtually real, more tempting
than reality, they are not ignored.
The poor fish, such a weak fish,
goes for the gold.

A snap and the hook is
lodged in his gullet.
He twists against currents.
His flesh pulls and tears.
He whips up the water.
The red froth surrounds him.
He thrashes his backbone
to rip himself free.

The harder he struggles,
the deeper the hook bites;
the more he is wounded,
the weaker he grows.

The fisherman puppets
will pull all the strings now.
They will consume him
(if he measures up).

The net that enfolds him,
the old world-wide net,
was waiting, was ready,
defined by the options
that others determined.
No salvage in reason.
No choices were his.

STRING

A woman named Pearl,
found hanging by her neck
from a gold wire,
dripped quicksilver fluids
into droplets that skittered over
the tile, stalking each other.

Small, yellow slickers glisten
on the cloakroom wall, pegged,
plastic wrappers guarding forlorn
mittens that cry for their mother.

Empty thumbs pile cartons
against the rush,
the brown water rush, that is a lie.
Truth is in the faceted ravines and
bouncing off my edges at precise angles
into safe pockets.
A huge stick splits the triangle:
balls are spewed in all directions.

A spinning compass begs me to follow
the gull that drops its mollusk on a rock.
Flying would have made all the difference.

The weight of globes is handheld.
Reality is pinned on a wall.
Being is a process now,
tubes in,
tubes out,
a survival meeting where
the organism strives only for breath.
It has come to that.

CIRCUS #1 – THE ANIMALS

Animal smells sharpen the air, tapping into my
consciousness through nostrils that flare to sniff.
Horses.
With pink-plumed manes and painted and polished
hooves, they prance wearing gaudy saddles and
silver-gilt reins that show worn leather
through the cracked folds.
Elephants.
Splotched, gray bulks sway from left to right on
plate-like feet planted firmly as they curl the hairy
pink ends of their trunks around the hooks of their mahouts.
Their skin will feel the bite of those hooks.
Tiger.
Exuding a strong cat odor, unable to hide his feces beneath
the scattered green straw mottled yellow by urine,
he crushes his padded feet onto the wooden boards,
pacing between the rows of iron bars.
Not to be teased or fed, he rises above the upturned faces.
His coat burns brightly in the sunlight.
Bears.
There are none here. There should have been European brown bears.
Perhaps they were forgotten and left behind in Europe.
Still wearing their silly hats and collars; they may have been
abandoned to stand on street corners in the cities.
Unloving people, full of fear fathered by ignorance,
would chase them. If a bear struck back, he would be shot,
executed, no fellow bears around to take his part.
One bear dead for one human frightened.
Bears would eventually be eliminated since
there are far fewer bears than humans.
No one to wash them, lick them clean, or pick them
free of lice, they would weave their heavy heads
back and forth,
eyes wide with childlike innocence,
eyes searching for a loving presence,
eyes brimming with bear tears

mourning their lost memories.
They would point their muzzles upward,
sniffing the animal smells that sharpen the air,
sniffing the smell of humans.

RADIO

Songs leak out of the old guitars and
slide like oil over the frets, gliding in
on radio waves from halfway around
the world. Coming from Mexico, Spain,
Nashville, Memphis, they are out of sync
with the rumble of rubber-rimmed wheels.

Patients finger their bandaged heads while
I.V. stands conduct needles into veins,
tracheotomies whistle as air moves in and out,
catheters pipe urine into plastic bags.
The guitar chords clash with gasps as
tired bodies struggle to breathe.
Arpeggios irritate muscles into
arrhythmic twitches from the
plucking of sympathetic nerves.

A knitted throw covers his atrophied legs.
They once neighbored mine.
We swayed together, held each other.
Sometimes it felt good, sometimes not.
Now I am the only visitor he has.
He grabs my hand and kisses it and says,
"I want to dance with you."

VII
Light Gasp from the Past
Mortality

LUCY

"The significance of Lucy is her completeness and her great age."

She is more than a skeleton,
an archaeological find.
She was a woman who must have
shuffled, hunched, arms dangling,
senses alert to unfamiliar
sights, to unknown smells,
sounds of nearing danger.

Her body belonged to the clan
to procreate, to replace
those who died young.
There were so many.

Sleep was brief, snatched in corners.
Hidden, fearful, alone.
Love for her children led
to weakness, daily sorrow.
Survival was primary,
forced the strong ones
into selfishness.

Her short life ended
by a brutal blow,
likely from a hostile clan, she fell,
laid there for millennia
blanketed by earth
until men dug up her bones.

Acclaiming their discovery,
giving thanks for her preservation,
her value for science,
they ignored her life story
the tragedy of her death, crowed:

Look how far we've come,
how much we've changed.

A DOOR OPENS

a door closes,
a woman descends the stairs
planning to navigate
the sidewalk,
resolved to dominate
the boulevard,
determined to challenge
the authority of vehicles,
forgets that she has
left her glasses at home.

Her legs are veined
with thick, blue ropes,
and a blurry hazard
made by children
or unleashed dogs
clogs the passage
to the end of the block.

A MINOR NOTE

The women sit.
They choose to chat.
A fugue of tongues
since no one stops
long enough
to listen to the others.

There was a time
I chimed in,
claimed membership
in the wedded female set,
the field of shared living.

Today, I sit,
watch the others.
He's too long dead,
my mildewed
memories—irrelevant,
will not be heard.

OUT OF MY DEPTH

Iridescent fish, crimson, orange, yellow,
        trimmed with delicate, translucent fins,
parrotfish in jewel tones, emerald blending
        into amethyst, swim next to me.
Sergeant-majors, black and white, tipped with
        gold, angelfish with arching fins, all gleam.
My astigmatic eyes, magnified by water and the
        claustrophobic mask, follow a pattern, a
continuous wall built of fish that seem to mesh,
        Escher-like, into each other's outlined forms.
I am connected by my plastic, umbilical snorkel
        to the surface, to my world.
My cupped hands pull the water, resisting, into
        my chest, then push it away to the rhythm
of the undulating current. Below, seaweed
        fans sway in the surge that carries me
farther away from shore. Long, bubbly strands of
        kelp tug at their anchors on the sandy bottom.
An eel pokes its thick body out from its rock-edged
        cave, gapes its jaws and alarms a
school of little silver anchovies. I reach out to
        touch a school of wrasse, but it shies and
darts away as though it were a single creature, so
        I follow it down to where the beams of light
grow dimmer, where the water begins to darken.
        It would be so easy to take a breath and let the
snorkel fill, so effortless to keep on going down.
        It is hard work to swim back to the beach,
to struggle against the powerful pulse of the water.
        I dog-paddle, lift my mask to peer at the dim
shoreline, a wavering mirage in the distance.
        I blow the snorkel clear, but my mouth
half-fills with brine and sears my throat.
        It is a battle to rediscover shore-bound waves.
I force my weary arms into one more stroke.

A WOMAN'S CHOICE

I helped her throw black netting over her loquat tree to keep the birds from eating all the fruit. Next to the trunk was the pile of birdseed she'd left for those same house finches. The black netting looked like a veil, with dots that reminded her of her cataracts. She was going to have them removed, she said, as soon as she could decide on a day.

Her other doctor had told her that the incision from the small node she'd had cut out was healing very well, they had gotten all the cancer cells, but he recommended radiation anyway. She refused. Her sister and her son tried to convince her, but she was adamant.

"I've lived for eighty-five years," she told me. "Suppose I do all this stuff—who knows what will happen? I could die in an accident, or in an earthquake, or choke on a fish bone. Radiation makes people feel weak and I want all my strength. What a fuss over such a tiny tumor."

She had things to do, ushering at a local theater, volunteer work, daily walks, meeting her neighbors, bringing them fruit from her garden. She wanted to keep visiting her grandkids, hear their stories about living in Europe or South America, places she will see only through their eyes.

"What if it spreads? What if you lose a breast?"

"Listen—I'm not nursing a baby. I don't plan to have a lover. When I visit my friends and neighbors, no one will know what I look like under my clothes. I've said it over and over, it's MY choice."

I wanted to tell her not to abandon me, not to leave me without her, but how could

I persuade her when her own son couldn't? I put my arms around her, feeling her close, and tried to will my body to memorize hers.

ACT THREE[5]

No one can remember
all of act one—it recedes
from memory, the scenes
run together, change
order, pawns of the pea-
under-the-shell shifts.

It was hopeful, act one,
that much I know,
ambitious, striving
for success and procreation.

Act two was growth,
the savoring of fruits newly tasted,
storing up for the future
without loneliness,
watching our children prosper, or not.

Act two is over.
It's time to rest on our laurels, regroup.
Holding hands during intermission,
we are awarded a respite
from the intricacies
of the plot.

Act three will be spare,
filled with apprehension.
The cast depleted,
we experience a different
kind of waiting.
Death is the new director.

---

5   Published in *Rattle*, Issue No. 20, December 2003.

AUTUMN IN NEW YORK

That year, trees clung to their leaves,
refused to release them, wouldn't let them fall.
The leaves turned
green to red to yellow to brown.
Spotted with dirt,
made ragged by insects,
they were held by the stubborn limbs.

Leaves themselves wouldn't let go,
stuck to the tight mother-glue
of green sap that nourished them,
some reached their potential,
some faced early demise.
All stubbornly held fast.

Men did not rake or mound
them. No children mashed
them into snapping,
crackling shreds.
That year limbs and leaves
held onto each other
in terror of hurtling down,
destruction by fire.

This winter, 2001 buried
in memory, the leaves
will release and drop,
baring the limbs.

AWAKENING

Fighting to be partner, not weak, dependent,
I iterated, spoke words louder, sieved
sentences through white teeth, set
like a picket fence guarding my open
mouth, pink tongue, searching not for
your pink tongue, but the earned response
to my need to hear, be acknowledged.
Desperation pushed me to write
my needs, my cares, thrusting into
your line of vision a yellow legal pad
with wet splotches where anger overflowed,
despair formal from me,
Mrs., addressed to your Mr.

Guilty, you said, of stealing your power,
nonexistent, my guilt gave you leave
to leave free of responsibility,
chains of our history, burdened
by years, were broken, enveloped
in denial, your favorite response
to challenges requiring insight and thought.

Devastated by our son's determination
to seek elsewhere for affirmation,
I dreamt of you, believed you were
there for me, listening as you never
had, caring as you never did. My sleeping
brain felt you would be there for me.
I woke, startling from sleep to desolate
abandonment. My sons and I burned
white sage to send your body purified
into the flame. We laid a layer of
ashes on your earthly resting places.

BIRD ON WIRE

Air pecking
> while his foot pad between bone-thin
> claws weaves his balance against

the slight wiggle
> of a perch in space,
> electric high wire show

without umbrella
> or bamboo pole, stability
> for a winged creature—extraneous.

His beak shoves
> under a wing to warm,
> fuzzy spots, probes

finds a mite, tiny bite.
> He needs much more,
> a spider, a worm banquet.

Hollow-boned, his body
> glides away unseen, above
> slow earth-bound bodies.

Above a hennaed gray-rooted coif,
> a balding scalp, remaining
> strands of hair combed over

in defiance, rebellion against—
> waning of youth,
> the burning pains,
> all the losses.

BIRD WAITING

Wings spread,
twiggy legs
thrust forward,
the egret lights
in the muck.
Its wings fold tight,
seamless, precise—
all motion freezes.

She watches
the egret, beak
poised to spear
any tiny fish,
the tension in its
S-shaped neck,
its concentration.
The force of hunger
in the bird
is stronger
than anything
she feels in herself.

CAREFUL WISHES

Bouquets of wishes
ribboned together
overwhelm the vases
left by visitors
to this antiseptic
room, yesterday,
a week ago,
flowers now
bereft of petals,
stems stripped of leaves.

Her dry eye blinks,
she dismisses
today's messages, cards
hallmarked, shoe-boxed,
dwells on the long ago
clink of wine glasses,
toasts to long life. She
remembers,
buried under
her octopus of restraints,
her caul of plastic piping.

AWARENESS

expands
from birth,
grows
into,
through,
past
family.

Fed, clothed,
taught the rules
of fenced-in playgrounds,
fear of strangers,
crossing streets,
and dirt.

Lacking riches,
immortal love,
I compromised,
breathed into my
middle-class mind
the pure air of me,
grew some more,
liked where I was.

I like it still,
and I will stay
for a while,
being me
so long as my
awareness
remains
intact.

CAT SCAN

How dare they peer
deeper than I can,
below my dermal
layers, interfibrillar scene,
bone discounted, bone
bound by ligament
and tendon?

Gurney slides through
a torus haloed with
incandescence, laser,
a warning label tells me
not to focus on light
or meaning, let them do it.
Trust their expertise.
I trust myself.

They hold more knowledge
of my body than I,
but they can never
hold my mind.

CROSSING OVER

Few riders marvel at the bridge,
its structure, its flaking skin
of orange rust, its wrist-thick cables,
the retinue of restorers, the visitors.

Someone stands close by the railing,
waiting to serve an insidious
commander, internal, insistent.
Staring down through tearing eyes,
he perches for a moment
on the railing, without birdlike
claws or wings, flies off.

Far below, the hard-surfaced ocean slams
the jumper into the end he thought he wanted.
If regret could call back deeds, he might
be the first to rewind the film, send
the spray backwards, up out of the water,
retrieve the irretrievable, lift to safety.

Maybe he sought the vortex Alice found,
hidden entrance into a fabled place
where a loner might find succor,
but he damned his body to destruction,
his mind to oblivion, may not
have found his paradise of peace.

If misery can no longer be endured,
sorrow, well and truly drowned,
will lose its stranglehold, cast off
the suffering body to be fished
out by vigilant boat patrollers.

A bridge-crosser, straining to see
the city, might still wonder
if he would have the courage/
cowardice to do the same.

DINNER PARTY

My earth-toned stoneware plates
anchor my second-best cloth.
My mother's silver plate, ornate,
initialed, a little worn in spots,
separates the settings. Guests
appear in ones and twos, hugs
all around, comments on how
well we all look, drinks until
we reach the table, toasts
are given, forks flash. Along
with half-joking slanders of
absent friends, the litany
of bravery, of ailing ones,
the food is praised, eaten.

So much time to prepare,
so quick to be consumed.
I carry plates coated
with dried sauce, a confetti
of dried green vegetables
into the kitchen, discard
a chipped glass, wilted flowers,
everything that is finished,
used, cracked. Clatter fills
the silence that descends
when guests leave. Hands
busy, my mind freed,
I remember other meals.
Fewer friends this time,
and these days, they go home early.

DOORKNOBS

More than storage for rubber bands,
wet towels, doorknobs turn, reveal
access to gardens, avenues, away
from interior stifling, turn
to let a person enter—someone
from the past—a long ago young
lover, sharing good times, going
to a bar to hear jazz, nurse a beer,
a Tom Collins for hours. He
didn't have a lot of money.
We married.

OR a more recent middle-aged
friend of years, a sudden lover,
a person of seductive world power,
hobnobber with A-listed people,
an attraction I could not resist.
He came despite his fear, liar
to his wife, liar to me,
liar to his own body; denying
mortality, he died.
I wept in secret.

OR today, I expect good people
outside my door, meaning
no harm, friendly, helpful,
and I feel the fool when
an evil one appears dealing
in trouble. I still throw open
the door and, like the long-time-ago
song of anti-war liberals,
when will I even learn?

EXHIBITION

Wearing gray and brown colors,
lightweight in her wheelchair, clutching
a loose woolen shawl, she enters.
Her skin papery, face drained of color
but for dark circles seen through her
glasses. In honor of her artist friend she needs

    to be here.

to see brilliant fabrics—exotic red embossed,
blue embroidered, sewn into open
umbrellas, draped hangings.
Vibrant, the exhibit pulses. Patrons,
fellow guests, a polyglot of showy
gallery hoppers, dress in wild attire

    to be here.

Artist friends she has curated hesitate
to kiss her, touch her hand, fearful
of bruising, or squeamish at illness
They hover, murmur (none say she
looks well). Her head droops, chair
moves, slowed by the throng invited

    to be here

Her good companion shepherds her
toward the door, leaving behind others
quick to turn away for another glass of wine,
another snack, closing their circle, resuming
conversations—the present exhibition,
achievements, gossip, plans.

    Ah, yes, to be here.

EXORCISM

I chanted while the white sage smoldered,
waved the bound leaves over and around
to push out specters, memories, free me,
as well as all the rooms, of burden.

The taut skull-tight faces of those
who did or did not still exist
had scuttled into the black holes
that swallowed light inside my mind.

My sons performed this ritual
around their father's body, felt
his spirit had spent many years
imprisoned in a useless frame.

Our tribe is old, dates back to Solomon;
our heritage has other cleansing rites,
but they chose this one, so I watched,
and, for my part, I stroked his wax-like face.

His spirit may have soared, for me
the burning of the sage did not succeed.
I moved away, to someplace new,
but all my hidden sorrows followed me.

FINAL CHOICE

Sitting on the front porch
memorizing license plates
had lost its challenge.
Cards folded away
from her hands,
and her fingers
had grown too small
to hold the days
together.

Salt and salsa
translated into bland
indifference,
each mouthful
a chore.

She needed a walker
for locomotion, a leaky
diaper pad for urination,
the day room TV set
for cogitation.

But, the end of fruitfulness,
that was worst of all.

She chose to stop living.

GENERATIONS

In sewing bees, a generation past,
women filled quilts, shared
advice, touched the truth
of pain, hugged each other.

Tonight, it's envelopes we fill
with warnings to our sisters
of threats to hard-won rights,
these twenty-somethings and me.

All have careers: counselor,
programmer, designer,
therapist. I don't tell them I'm
retired, or what I used to do.

They talk of travel:
Scotland, with parents;
Israel, with a student group.
I have been to Timbuktu,
Madagascar, Borneo. I say nothing.

They chatter about plans for tonight.
One to meet a boyfriend;
another, a foreign visitor,
go dancing in Hollywood.
I will not proclaim,
I'm going home.

DARK SPRING

A cool breeze steals the warmth the
sun had radiated earlier as it stole
the dampness from the flowers, the
dew from the grass. The furrowed
earth is striped with outlines of old
wetness, like a wrinkled cheek discolored
by the courses of dried tears.

Carrion birds, bereft of song, sail out with
wings spread full, with feathered fingers
separated, outlined black against the sky.
In silent flight they circle, hover, ever
closer to the ground, then land near a
small body. They will leave behind
a brainless skull, a centerpiece of bones.

Lilies, topping leafless stalks, punched
upward from their bulbs just yesterday.
The countdown starts for them the minute
they open to the light. Tomorrow they
will brown and shrivel, bending over
helpless, drained by time.

Crows mock with unmelodic
raucous shrieks the light, bright air.
My dog no longer sees the light,
no longer hears the crows,
but she knows something comes
to brush her cheek, caress her muzzle,
covering the gray with long,
black strokes of wings.

DAWN

Some dawns, a staccato clamor
breaks open the oyster shell
of sleep. It is short, like the
rounded steel blade, but long
enough to pry me out, to
spread the lips of my comforter,
the sole warmer of my bed.
The forlorn telephone bleat may
be an omen of fearful news,
an augury of sorrow, but I must
honor the imperative to answer
and to listen.

A woman torn between peace and pain
and not allowed to make a choice,

a man so thrust into his battle to survive,
he lost the ability to nurture love,

a friend, struck by the modern plague,
the scourge of the end of the 20th century,

the child that I bore and loved and wished
the best for, needing my hand one more time,

my freedom from a duty that I do not want
to a person that I ceased to love years ago.

On other dawns I wake to still
darkness under the first tentative
ray of light. In my silent bedroom, I
stare at the telephone and will it
to ring. History must be concluded,
final dates must be stamped.
This might be the day.

FREE WILL

Chairs around the table
in this center—rehab for some,
residence for these—
each pair of eyes unfocused,
a gape or a grimace,
set, unmoving, until
stirred by another,
as a coin slotted to turn
a mechanical person ON;
when fixed mouths
shape-shift, twist.

Wanting, hunger eat up the air.
Impulse shared, all obey.
Safety in confinement,
a pin closes up a shirt.
Nested, separated
by wheels that touch, and only wheels.
Do not touch a stranger!
Do not discuss!

If each has a goal,
it is to survive another day.
Or, having no goals at all,
mere existence.
They cannot choose to leave
the group of their own free will.

GHOST TOWN

Identical bungalows, broken metal
lath poking through pastel stucco
corners, line up double-file, their
sagging yellow roofs staggered

like chevrons. Grey-brown barrack
walls age to silver, so do barricaded
doors, grimy windows. Sentries
gone, the metal gates are locked down.

Survivors—wives, husbands,
kids who chased the mailman—
have shipped out, gone to another
base or to renewal of civilian life,

freed from the wait for a dreaded letter
or visit from an officer. No one now
parades down the streets of this town,
except a procession of military ghosts.

GOD'S MESSAGE

Will it penetrate the Van Allen belt—this signal
from a fragile, plastic cellphone—flipped open,
aimed skyward, relayed from an earth conduit
to a stalking satellite and upward, outward?

I hear the chimes, they sound heavenly,
mellifluous, an original composition. What
shall I say to him—in English, of course?
He will be sympathetic, understand my

dilemma—my need to be rich, successful
yet caring, concerned about all those
other people. He will surely help me in one
of my hours of need for investment insight.

Didn't I dedicate my first and second born
sons to be tutored in his word, to respect,
revere him, take his word as gospel, attend
his house on holidays when there is time?

The chiming ends and a voice sounds in my inner ear,
I'm sorry, I can't come to the phone right now . . .

SOUNDS

The radio brings in a welcome voice,
filling the spaces in the air
like plastic inserts in a package—
don't let the contents rattle, something might break—
and sound is the shield to use.
Reporters, commentators, best of all music,
quiet chamber groups, rhythmic pop with harmless lyrics,
never the whining, lost-loving, dying-without-the-irreplaceable-sweetheart
words of country-western, but the smooth, gentle waves
flowing right into my head through earphones.
Worn even into bed, the sound
spreads out into the pathways
where dreams are drawn,
black and white outlines waiting to be filled in
like painting by numbers.
The noise from outside is the brush,
the notes of the music provide the colors.
I want no choice for my brain
but pleasant dreams.
I can fool it into thinking it is happy,
and sometimes when a speaking voice breaks in,
into feeling that there's actually
another human being lying next to me.

HATS[6]

She began with a perky hat,
natural straw, open weave,
an orange feather tucked
into a band of zig-zag design.

As her hair thinned, she turned
to gentle denim, a soft drape
comforting like flannel sheets.
Under wide brims, she found

protection from harsh light,
camouflage for sunken
cheeks, dark circles. Then
she discarded all the hats,
wore the grey stubble of her hair
with pride and defiance.

Today, filing past her coffin,
we throw flowers to celebrate
her life, a handful of stones
to bind her body to the earth.

A rush of wind, sudden, fierce,
tore off my hat, sailed it high.
I could see her wearing it,
her hair loose and full
and shining in the sunlight.

---

6   Published in *White Pelican Review*, October 2004.

EMERGE

An unborn writhes, flexes,
cradled in fluid until
pushed down, forced out
through slippery,
convulsing flesh,
expelled into air,
while family,
deep into a birth fugue,
emotional, apprehensive,
pause to breathe,
relieved at news
of the delivery.

Another, unhatched,
is cramped inside its shell,
warmed under
soft plumage until
it pecks hard,
breaks out of confinement
to where feathers can dry,
where poets wait to set
lyrics to the music
of chirping and twittering.

Human, avian,
emerge,
outraged at expulsion,
screaming
for sustenance, for attention,
fearing daylight,
the vast outside.

I AM STILL WOMAN

Responsive to the touch of lips,
fingertips, I felt loved,
bore three sons. Proud as I presented
them to their father, I triumphed—a woman.
The bits of cells they left behind at birth
stayed buried in my flesh. Nursing
them, my womb contracted,
cycle womb-breast-womb. Now

the oval berries on my internal vine,
storage pods for new life, the womb
that was the birth vessel, all pruned,
discarded, leaving stumps
that will not regenerate.
Altered but staunch,
still female,
a mother, I stake my claim
to all rewards and perils
of womanhood.

OLD PIPES

Rust eats old pipes.
Those carriers
of vital liquids
leak around worn
joints.
Scales flake off
into chaff towers,
under pitted surfaces.

My pipes
fall victim,
thin from age,
decay from the
rust of years.

PLUTO SPACE

Pluto, the ninth "planet," lost
its title, but some space is still there.

I should start up something
to take advantage of the endless
view from the edge of space
with a platform of relevant objects
for the universe to receive:
my ether mails,
my attachments to the Milky Way,
my link-ups with all the
unreachable galaxies.

Communications will take
longer than a googol of lifetimes
before an unforeseen egg
in an unborn woman could
evolve to hear the answer
of a yet-to-be-created,
unwritten question.

JETTY

Walking the jetty toward the west, I trace Catalina's outline,
the humps of the hills, the slender waist of the isthmus,
a sight that is clear only after winter rains or winds.

The view toward the east is special today.
New snow has turned the ridges
into elderly guardians of the basin.
Aloof and stern, there are no warm hugs
from these old mountain men and women.

Last summer, my sons and I came here to cast ashes into the ocean.
Warm weather particulates laid a veil between us and the mountains,
between us and the island.

We settled on this place anyway for what it might mean
to a man who had enjoyed mountains, beaches, and sea.
We chose a spot beyond the rocks
where the water seemed calm.

The heavy ashes formed a pillar.
Filmy at first, then becoming thicker,
they made a link between the visible floor of the ocean and its surface.
We lingered by the pillar, watched it for a while;
it swayed with the current but did not disperse.

Today, the water is muddy, stirred up by the wind.
I can't see the bottom, there below the rocks,
but I can see the mountains, the island,
the clouds softening the sky.

JIGSAW PUZZLE

My guide is the box-top picture,
a blurry Renoir copy.
This portrait of a pink-cheeked girl,
her long tresses,
her dress of white chambray,
is bathed in an impressionistic glow.
Her hazel eyes are tinged with green like mine,
but unlike mine,
hers are calm, passive, waiting.

I turn the pieces face up, align
the straight-edged ones, the corners first.
Compelled to work within the border,
I match background leaf
to background leaf, fit bits
of blue sky into the proper pockets.

I fret.
I want to push into the center,
get to the heart of the puzzle,
but I am constrained to follow
the order I learned:
work from the outside in.

This was the only way to solve puzzles,
my mother insisted, until one day,
I screamed in my eight-year-old voice,
        "Get away, don't bother me,
        I don't need your help."

I didn't want to be or look like her,
but every day now,
when I brush my teeth
or comb my hair,
I see her muddy skin;
her wrinkles line my forehead,

pucker my neck,
ladder up my cheeks.

Now, I rebuild the girl's
smooth rosy face—fresh and unlined.

I find her eyes and fit them in;
they watch me, fixed,
without emotion.

Her lips are pink and smiling.
A few teeth show, but there's
no tongue behind them.

Her long brown hair glints
with highlights. Golden,
they will never turn to gray.

I fit in all the parts I have,
but the girl is incomplete.
Someone's taken one piece,
or it's lost.
She must remain
what she always was:
not quite whole.

LACY LEAF

Like a lacy lady slimmed to a shade,
with skin thinned to near transparency, easy to tear,
bones worn to brittle, easy to break.
Joints protest, spine stiffens.
Age, the terrorist, is acknowledged—rejected.

Her spirit, full, alive, is as it was except—
her day starts a little later,
gingerly, fewer exercises before
more leisurely dressing
in attractive trousers or skirt.

Mirror time, a little longer today,
more makeup covering basal cell scars,
gray-blonde wig adjusted,
jewelry selected,
memories selected; mascara must not run.

She leaves her room to join her guest,
discuss her plan for a farewell
to herself. She claims she wants
to see who shows up,
what they say about her.

LAST PERFORMANCE

His hands float, pillowed on sound,
slide sideways, drift down
like snowflakes in a
paperweight globe, his touch
so soft, listeners hold
a collective breath.

I close my eyes, imagine
I see his fingers flex,
flick upward with the rhythm.
His arms fly up, crash
down, a thunderclap
of chords and arpeggios
that connect the centuries
from gaslight to electric
chandeliers, connect the
years from my youth
to middle age through
memories rising out of
despair to tearful rejoicing.

He ends, exhausted, bows
to the ovation, wipes his brow.
He cannot stop the tremors
of his hands across his face
or the shaking of his arms
as he acknowledges us.

Past and present merge.
Last year it was another
perfect concert when I cried.
This time I know—we all know—
he will never play for us again.

MODERN NAIAD

Past the swimming pool, its bubbling chemical froth,
our germicidal protection from each other, she descends
the staircase, wearing a barely-there bikini, disdains
the lounges, plotzes on the cement surface—padless.

Accoutrements: munchies, cell phone, soda
(Styrofoam cup) magazine (glossy).
No sign of sunscreen!
Has she not been terrified by infomercial threats,
warnings designed to shock, scare, sell products?
She flips. Full frontal presentation to burning rays.

Bikini—maybe at age 14 I could have worn one,
not been allowed to leave the house. I wore
a hand-me-down, one-piece, dirty yellow suit,
suffered under the sun, ears scorched by boys' comments.

A bikini today offers my voluptuous Maja-like
corpus fractional protection from the desiccating,
wrinkle-producing sun, leaving merciless light
as the sole serious threat to the rest of me.

She stands to leave, reveals her prominent
bony ribs, knobby knees, splayed feet.
Ah, so I breathe deep, smile a small pleased smile.

MOON

Plastic slats of blinds slice the moonlight into strips
          lunasticks

Enameled window sills, polished glass, turn moon-rays into flashing
  whirligigs
          lunaparks

Silver patterns the ocean which rolls its belly to a Debussy air
          Clair de Lune

A spotlight moon is fringed by flitting art deco clouds
          lunarians

Beating waves bare the gums of the shoreline
          lunar tides

Moon-lens closes its eye, shutters itself away from me.
          I drowse with the lunar ebb.

MY BODY IS A STATUE

My body is a statue,
flesh between
sun and
shadow.

The strands of my hair
are diffused by the light
of a mote-ridden cloud,
a disquieting halo.

When I move,
my shadow follows.
Light on its feet,
it flits and dances,
schitzy,
a Peter Pan
pasted to the soles
of my feet.

My lover,
a devil in his own right,
embraced my body,
acknowledged my shadow,
but missed my soul,
which he couldn't fathom
and couldn't buy.

NO FISHING

They stand, two men, exhaling smoke
into the wind, fishing rods propped
against the tubular metal barrier
against the sign, NO FISHING.
This is my spot I think, silent,
watching. This is where my sons
and I cast out my husband's ashes.

Oceans always drew him.
His wide torso well suited for body
surfing, he swam way out beyond
me into deeper, flatter water,
hung out and caught a likely wave,
curled into it, rode it back
in a blanket of foam.

Then, a different destination,
his ashes formed into a pillar
of gray, dropping to the bottom
of the channel, anchoring his spirit
to the ocean floor, swaying, drifting
into moving currents, leaving behind
painful memories, a needed relief.

Years after forgiveness,
sucked into a bubble of separation,
I sit alone on the jetty
where fishermen can't see what
lies below, what they might snag:
a purse, a toy, a wedding ring.
The sign means what it says.

DOVES

Soft grey, a pair of doves,
brown-spotted chests,
gentle coos, acrobats in slow
airs above the ground,
peck at seeds or tiny insects
barely visible next to leaves.

At my son's marriage,
in southern Mindanao,
doves were released at the
reception, traditional
white ones, pampered
for this occasion, to circle
briefly around the room,
then disappear to the
approval of the guests.

The grey doves here must
search and peck for their
survival, dismissed as
ordinary, forgettable birds.
In some places they are
killed for sport, shot
one after the other,
bodies falling to earth.

NOT A PHOENIX

When our last son moved away,
I felt abandoned.
Born of desperation, I
dreamt of you,
a dream I had not had for years.
For a solitary moment
you were there
listening as you never had,
caring as you rarely did.

My drifting brain, startled
from sleep into confusion,
felt bereft against all reason.
In the real world, my sons
and I had burned white sage,
sent your body purified
into the flames, where crackle
and smell rose together.

We laid a layer of ashes
over your earthly resting places
and measured out a trail
of residue down
into an ocean bay
deep enough
that no ghost remains.

ONE SHOE

Traffic lanes fill up, shut down.
Cell phones send important news,
another freeway fiasco. I tap
the steering wheel, punch
radio buttons, drag my eyes
from a dented hubcap to metal,
bits of glass in the outside lane.

There's a shoe, laces untied,
gaping open, abandoned.
A runner's shoe, black
with white dashes, a man's,
a woman's? I imagine
injury, someone in a blanket
bundled into an ambulance,
sirens whining, shoe forgotten.

I'm staring, wasting precious
time, keeping other drivers
away from shops, hair
salons, gymnasiums.
I leave the shoe behind,
now twice abandoned.
Its owner won't return,
and I will not remember.

ONLINE

From: Earthlink
To: Friends

Latest is the doctor's try at something new; it might be just the thing.
I came back from Colorado, altitude too much. Even with the oxygen,
not worth the strain. I hope I can go back some day.

From: Earthlink
To: Friends

I went to get a manicure today. Jean came by to drive me,
and the kids came, too. They're growing up so fast, and I want to watch.

From: Earthlink
To: Friends

No—don't come over. My hair—what's left of it—is a mess and no calls.
I love to talk, but I keep running out of breath. Keep sending
cards, though, and email is even better—I can answer back.

From: Earthlink
To: Friends

Don't come over. Did I say that already? I can't remember.
Sometimes now the days and nights get turned
around and just run into one another. How long has it been?

From: Earthlink
To: Friends

They have another treatment to try. The last, but then, who knows . . .

From: Earthlink
To: Friends

We were interrupted. A glitch—they kicked me off,

but I'm back on. I'm not ready to get off. Why does
that happen? Are they trying to get rid of me?

From: Earthlink
To: Friends

So beautiful outside, I can see the boats and the sun.
I haven't been out since the last doctor appointment—
last week or last month or whenever it was.

From: Earthlink
To: Friends

Sorry it's been so long—someone told me it's been a while
since I wrote you. Feeling so-so. Getting up a little. Kids
visited, but had to go back home—not sure where—back home.
They couldn't stay any longer.

From: Earthlink
To: Friends

Now they have to lift me all the time. Helper here
can't do it anymore. I have to go somewhere else, they say. I have
to go. My children are finding me a place. Goodbye to you all.

Hit file.

Hit close.

Hit disconnect.

ORIGAMI LESSON

Gold-embossed planets,
blue stars on crimson
squares, colorful creatures
emerge from the paper folds;
wings expand,
feet flatten,
heads peak
into a beak, turn
on a thin neck.

Elders, whose clever
hands began in childhood
to fold the birds, show
respect for their nature,
teach the delicate art,
adoption of its discipline,
          each fold razor sharp,
          exact to the next fold,
          every step ordered,
          unchangeable,
          produces

a precise line of cranes,
identical blessings:
live long,
be happy.

OZ

He wears a beret, cover
for a bald spot speckled
with brown blemishes,
blotchy legacies of the
eighty-ness of his years.

His eyes, wrinkled brow
show confusion. He cannot
fathom why young ones,
deaf to his wisdom, flock
to follow the same
unrewarding paths
he rejected more years
ago than they have lived.

They see a mere man
behind the curtain,
search for a new,
more inspiring, wizard.

PALE DISK

A pale disk hangs in the sky,
black draperies enclose
it, hang in folds, soften
the sharp circumference.

The features of a man
are proved by my imagination.
His skin looks pock-marked,
but I remember it as smooth
to my fingers once they
got beyond the beard.

My memory defaults—
I can't recall the desire
to touch, to kiss, to mold
my body against his, boldly.

My need to be cherished
bound me to him, forcing
my eyes to focus on a façade.

He left without remorse.
The anguish I felt has fled,
leaving gratitude
for forgetfulness.

I watch his features change,
become unrecognizable,
melt into the surface
of the pale disk
hanging in the sky.

PAPER BIRD

A paper bird,
deceptive in its fragility,
soars upward
on its brief voyage
only to fly back again
without a voice
to tell us what is hidden
out there.

Each time we send it off,
it returns more tattered,
with crumpled paper wings.

So we repair the body,
realign the wings,
straighten the tail,
send it aloft once more.
It crashes at our feet,
a ragged remnant.

We must feed it to the fire.
Let it flare, release
into filmy feathers
of a near-transparent grey.
We try to catch the ashes
as they float skyward,
deceptive in their fragility.

PARADE

His six-foot frame unbalanced by
one thick-soled shoe, his full upper
body, heavyweight, pushes forward
grabbing a walker, step-pause-step.

Facial muscles tense, willing
connection—brain to body—striving
to restore his slouched but unfettered
pace lost over years to nearly bone on bone.

A therapist clutches his belt. If he
falls, she is too slight to anchor him.
Third in line, his tiny wife pushes
a wheel chair for emergency.

His scientific mind forces his body
toward achievable goals. His wife
longs for return to younger days. Her
hope persists, but it is leaking away.

PATIO

Futureless, plastic birds fixed
within a square concrete shell
stand harpooned among red
and orange blossoms; robin
with windmilling wings, beak
flapping, feckless in the breeze;
faux canary, black-winged, helpless
in its sway below real, fluttering leaves.

Trapped in aging flesh, men, women
stare, watch the birds, glimpse a face,
familiar from long ago? A distant
place? Or here, this morning?
Each follows the one ahead, needing
to keep his place in line.

Some, aware of their environment,
thrive in a way, strive to reach
the wider world, overcome fear,
fatigue, move around the planter
with wheelchairs or canes,
circling again and again, getting ready.

POPPIES

Yesterday the poppies burned
orange, made luminous by rain
that scrubbed leaves clean.
Today strong winds batter
and force them to bow,
bend closer to the earth.

Poppy petals furl, as though
delicate sheaths could keep
gritty sand from invading
each bloom. I cover my face
with a cloth to screen out
dust and airborne viruses,
but poisons riding on the ether
invade my eyes and ears,
and these linger in my mind.

I picture poppies burgeoning
miles beyond our purple lupine,
in a desert climate similar
to this, but I see those clumps
of orange volunteers sprout
in furrows between long rows
of freshly covered graves.

RAGS[7]

bring memories of cloth diapers,
worn thin, used to polish glass;
T-shirts, logos faded, armpits
full of holes, turned into dusters.
Flannel shirts, buttons torn off,
were better than white dressy ones
that starch had made too scratchy.

Rags bring history. A drummer marched
beside his flag, his head bound up.
Soldiers, wearing blue or gray, used
tourniquets to stop the flowing blood.
Housebound women braided rags
into rugs for every colonial room.

Living brings me worn out sheets, pillow
cases, stringy towels. I pile them against
a leaking window to hold back cold
rain water, use them to wipe up spills,
clean the floor of dirt or muddy tracks.

After years of use a rag will fall apart,
and I give up a memory, a shred of life.

7   Published in *the Kerf*, College of the Redwoods, Summer 2005.

REALITY NIGHTMARE

Red lights swivel, flash; sirens,
harbingers of ill luck, wail
louder as they approach,
respond to urgent calls
from somewhere in this building.

Neighbors shiver in gowns,
robes, frightened awake
by screams at this scary hour.
Paramedics rush the elevator,
push the opening door,

emerge again with their
patient still screaming—
their meds aren't working—
everyone's worst nightmare.
Rapid wheeling of a gurney

through light into shadow,
going below to an ambulance.
The screams leave with him,
uneasy quiet returns.
The night seems blacker now.

REBIRTH

Insulated from the blood-chill
of the early summer ocean,
I ride inside a submersible,
a new machine but more secure
than unprotected scuba gear.
The protruding belly where I sit
reminds me of the gunner's
bubble of a B-52. I lurch
as the vessel shakes, descends
below the surface, makes
waves below waves.

The machine hovers above
the ocean floor, pokes its nose
into the crotch of the kelp.
Fronds above wave back and forth
as sinuous as the kimono sleeves
of a Chinese opera diva, as they thrust
olive-green pods toward the sun.

I breathe inside a reverse aquarium.
Inches thick, the plastic bulges
out into a fish world in miniature.
Schools of mackerel look like sardines.
Garibaldi are orange dots and move
in circles. Spotted bass, perch,
señoritas, opal eyes, are all
in shades of grey and black.

Tiny creatures cling to each other.
Light diffuses through their
near-transparent bodies.
They fuse into a mirror-like sheath
that joins with others to make
a curtain of shivering planes.
Motes of sand swirl with the current.

The water becomes a little
more opaque as we descend.

Eons ago, in the soup of the sea,
tiny bits came together, wriggled,
danced, and coupled
their way into a new atmosphere.

I see bubbles rising up from
the machine through the sea's fluid.
No umbilicus attaches me to the surface.
The liquid is the medium
through which the ship sways
in deliberate exploration.
My fate is in the hands
of oceanic gods and the diver
who guides the ship from outside.

I was born out of a place like this,
helpless, even then, in a windowless
darkness. My sense of it lurks
just behind memory's façade.
I chose to return here to feel
the rocking, the cradling
of the nurturing ocean,
to savor the silence
of salt-loving companions,
to see what divers see.

When the vessel surfaces
and the bubble opens,
I will be released into the upper world,
only this time it will be without pain.

RESTORATION

A castle built to stand for millennia
faced terror riding horseback, armored
as Teutonic knights who distorted pagan
practices with Christian dogma, tortured
then burnt heretics, plundered, ruined
the castle, dismantled its cannons.

Wars slowed, allowing natives seeking
their heritage to rebuild the castle,
historic home, to stand for millennia.
Its façade restored with bricks too new,
the cobbled courtyard without broken
stones, the turrets crowned with perfect tiles.

One original window's wavering
glass reflects my face, its lines,
its wrinkles, what a stranger sees.

The castle, doubly risen, projects
an image that imagination
by itself cannot provide.
So joints can be replaced, bones
reconstructed, skin made smooth and fresh.

I wish for more,
my youth restored.

ROLLING STOCK

Wailing, the train whistle cuts
through dawn-light, bays
toward covering clouds,
invites me to enter, wraps
in generous steel arms.
Protection has a price.
I must stay the predetermined
course, herded by rails.

Whooshing, we whisk by
standing, graffitied boxcars.
They leave me their names—
Burlington Northern,
Santa Fe, Union Pacific,
slab sided metal
carriers, beloved
by spray can addicts.

Poplars, sycamores,
larch, line up immobile.
It's the forest trees,
axed down, that float
into sawmills
to be sliced, crunched,
leave fiber piles
scattered by winds.

Skeletal trestles, marinas,
dredges, houseboats
on the Willamette
or the ocean intrusion
into the sound, find
moorings in the channels,
limited by cliffs, beaches,
shifting sand bars.

Then—
wisp of freshness,
wheeling herring gulls,
cormorants on piers,
hawks on pointed poles,
squirrels on flat ones,
fliers, jumpers, chasers
in need or in fear.

For me, the swaying
side to side is as close
to freedom as I get.
No one crosses first.
We start together,
end together.

I thought adventure,
new experience,
was the lure of travel
but on this limited trip
destination wins.

SEA CEREMONY

She wanted her ashes buried at sea
along with a glass of wine.

Dockside, waves cradle the moored boat.
We board, cast off, chug through
the channel, this voyage too purposeful
for reefing, into the rough Pacific,

gentler today, few whitecaps, low waves.
Quick turn, shoreward glance, a haze of houses,
fuzzy mountains beyond our grey-green
opaque surrounds. We stop.

The casket of ashes, in a basket
of flowers, lowered by rope
down and down again, fathoms deep
until it stops, is released.

The boat circles, crosses the wave line,
forms the symbol for infinity.
Over the burial spot, a bottle
is uncorked, wine poured.

A subdued motoring back into the marina.

       A cell phone rings, for him.
       A voice says, "thank you."

Another ring, another call, for him.

       "I need another glass of wine."

SHRINKING THE "BIG C"

This is it.
Rays have hit and hit again.
The target shrivels, does not disappear.

Days slip forward,
crimson roses spread, drop petals,
fragrant, munched on
by little green worms.

Acrobatic birds swoop, follow
a flight path, flash over drivers
who buzz through streets,
weave in and out of white lines,
the parallel confinement
focused on time and destination.

Sitting at the window,
her inner thoughts leak away,
slow, apprehensive, fearful
of pain, to count another day
as one more day to feel
the world spin, solitary,
even with the comforting
presence of friends.

SPRING SEA

Huge swells burst onto land.
Houses rip apart.
People sucked of life,
swallowed by spring sea.

He saw his children's smiles
early at breakfast.
Eager, ready
for school.

Tonight, he wanders
aimless and bereft.
He cannot
picture their faces.

SWIMMING BACKWARDS

Left arm circles up, back, pulls.
Right arm circles up, back, pulls.
I swim backwards, focus
skyward through dark goggles.

High above, an icy jet trail
marks passage of a metal
cocoon, a few hundred people,
pupae for now, nurtured
by hovering hosts while I am

thousands of feet below. In
the levels of space between
glide the natural fliers, one
great blue heron, pair of mallards,
flock of gulls. I stare way past them

to the heavens where the man-made
hull substitutes as god. All aboard
need faith their bodies are protected,
release their spirits to spurt ahead
to real-time destinations. I imagine

the ports they may aim for, recall
travels in the plush and plastic seats,
the peripatetic watchers who reacted,
in resignation or relief, to the changing
dictates of the seatbelt signs.

Panther-paced stewards walk the aisles
willing silence for silence's sake.
Passengers, restless mummies
wrapped in thin blankets, solicit
sleep for cheerful dreams,

find tenuous ones of travelers
met long ago, names
forgotten, faces fleetingly
constructed, familiar
just in ragged memories.

I hold such memories in my mind
as water holds my length ungrounded,
lifted in wet space, bounded by
four tile walls. Chemicals protect
me, circulators flow water in and out

preset thermostats warm my coldness
until I leave the amniotic lull,
experience my body, heavy, tied to
gravity, cast back to self-reliance,
my own earth-bound existence.

TANGOS AND MORE

The music of violin, viola, cello
resonates, swells, glides over
traditional into the sensual
dance music of Latin America,
then wow, the composer
astonishes us, casts us into
klezmer, its wept-over
wail, its rising, plunging beat.

I vibrate, measure rhythm
with my feet. My knees bounce,
shoulders shake. My mind
dances while my hips shift
on the padded pew bench.

The startling switch from
tango-based Argentinian
to klezmer is welcomed
in this sanctuary below
the staggered organ pipes,
the unadorned cross.

Inside this church, I feel
an ancient Hebraic sensibility,
the flavor of Eastern Europe,
out of shtetls into dances,
weddings, births/brisses,
the triumph of life beyond
the persecution of pogroms.

THE ALBUM

Ragged-edged, woven paper
pokes out beyond the cover,
so does one grainy sepia
photo from the forties,
her wedding suit ivory linen,
his uniform khaki. Smiling,
they gaze at each other.

A group picture—his father,
mother, two brothers; when
she married him, she married
them. He's dressed here
in a professorial suit.

Small group of photos
of their only son, as infant,
teenager, college grad.

Programs pasted in—West Coast
opening of Oklahoma, a concert
in Los Angeles, a showing
of *Ninotchka*, Garbo's film,
in downtown Montreal,

the rest empty, yellowed vellum.
He'd set aside this album,
retrieved it for today, sixty years
after photo number one.

His eyes meet ours, gauge
our interest; hers look
unfocused, empty. She has
forgotten us, her oldest friends,
but she knows he's there,
holds his hand.
Smiling, he gazes at her.

THERE IS A TIME

The edge of the wind will dull
when it curls around the loosened
pack of ashes. The knife of the
wind will not slice but crumble
the loaf, scattering ashes into
the needy mouth of earth.
None will fall in even rows,
planted like onions or corn
to ensure a crop of clones,
a replacement harvest like
the soldiers who sprang from
the dragon's teeth that
Cadmus sowed. This man's image
will shuttle in the wind's weft
from brain cell to brain cell,
each pattern unique.

The obituary listed times and
places, dates and obligations,
honors and accomplishments,
but it did not reach out to them
as his hands did, to grasp theirs
in congratulation for a problem
well solved. Armored by their
still fabric suits, their precise
remembrances, they stand to
tell of the emptiness he leaves
in the places where he touched them.

Target of their love for all their lives,
his children placed him in the eye of
the concentric circles. They honor and
praise him, the father/god, although
his expectations were their sometimes
failed goals. Today they lead
THEIR children back to him

Not every one
of your
lovers will
find her
voice today,
in this place.
Women move
on and lose
their connection.
Women hurt,
encapsulate
feelings and
transfer
their affections
to a different
embrace.

I may not
have been your
first love, but
I was your last.
Chosen after many
years of knowing
each other, you
cherished me
as a major
augmentation
to your life.

Now, I imagine
your body
sliding down a
bank into the
river, where
the black soil
crumbles

in memories to help them find a
protected place from which to
peer out at this unsettling scene.

Cars roll in, delivering those who
knew his unwillingness to surrender,
even to fist-clenching pain. Faces,
family or familiar, focus on each other,
their eyes circled with fatigue,
their glasses spotted by eyelash-flicked
tears, unwelcome drizzles, dampening
corners of mouths that came prepared
to smile and find it difficult.

The mute widow touches hands,
offers her cheek, receives embraces.
She monitors the music a child
performs, a poem another reads
and nods at the eulogies.
Appalled by the threat of self
disclosure, she bounces her thoughts
off cranial walls, wraps them in
blankets, smothering cursed sounds.

Those who can, speak.
Those who cannot, teach
the others LISTENING, the
gift of hearing. They hear
paeans of closure,
or pithy phrases
crafted to console.

His ears are stopped.
The jaws of nature
clamped shut, grinding
down on the music of his
words, the drama of his
humanity, the arias of
his life, spitting out the essence
from which a new unfettered
world will shape itself for him.

after you, your
fingertips barely
evading mine.

The pebbles
that pave
the stream
bed reflect
light into
a fish-scale
pattern
that drifts
upward.

I see you
floating,
loose-limbed,
downstream.
Mouth-gaped
but voiceless
you peer up
toward
the sky.

Your body
light and silent,
trails weed
wisps out
to a place
where the river
mouth fans out.

My love is not
a net, or if it is,
it is not strong
enough to
hold you. Your
arms are too
slippery to
carry me away
with you.

This is the reason and this
is the time for celebration.

Goodbye.

THE GREEN LINE

Hooked up to the machine, I track
a green line as it rolls out,
a lime-colored crack,
a sine-waved continuous stretch
across a Cartesian grid,
pulsing through black lacquer.

My heart beats, a needle moves.
A life-affirming machine,
but my body is the true wonder,
a workable design, developed
over eons, adapted to survival
by evolving outside forces.

No machine can measure
affection, hope, regret,
emotions the ancients
claimed were centered
in the human heart,
the yogi heart chakra.

Beyond dead lovers, lost
children, forgotten friendships,
the heart still beats,
the green line continues,
even through struggles
for breath. All the machine
needs is a living patient
and a source of energy.

THE PLUNGE

At night the lifeguard towers
loom—leggy, ghost-like, blue
cranes—not a place for shelter,
the cops look there first,
prowl the beach, trap fugitives
with the blinding beams
of powerful searchlights.

We run fast into blackness,
ankles wobbling in loose sand,
and hit the water's edge.
We giggle, naked, shiver,
duck into the freezing
surf. Thrilled by danger,
by fear, I feel the water
twist my body. Without
my glasses I can see
nothing but fuzzy lights
wavering in the distance.

I grab my husband, my hand
slides off, I plunge backward
downward, pummeled
by invisible waves. I stagger
out, dash to dry myself,
breathless to escape
before the patrol spots us.

I stand, cry out, terrified,
needing him there,
but, blinded, I can only
wait for him to find me.

THE RING

Blazing hot, the top layer of sand
fries the soles of my feet. I flop
down onto a couch of towels,
nestling into the loose sand
as it mounds beneath my breasts.

Sunlight, brilliant, relentless,
translates into shadows
behind my eyelids, drags
shreds of a dark fog across
my languid summer afternoon.

Ears buzzing with the soft rush
of warm breezes mixed with
the muted slush of breaking waves,
I feel a sudden cold wind,
the prickle of gooseflesh.

Talking couples, shrieking kids,
cellphones, seem as remote
as if behind a glass wall. In a daze,
my fingers sift through bits
of shell, cigarette butts, bottle

caps, down to a damper layer
a shade below the sun-loved
surface. A sudden move, I lift
my finger, my ring is gone.
my wedding ring, plain gold,

twin to the one my husband
refused to wear. I have lost it.
I cry out, then realize,
sucked down into shifting sand,
it has vanished beyond reclaiming.

THE THIN MAN

skin stretched over prominent
bones, trots along the shore,
wavelets puddling on the sand,
seeking a wave-packed solid
footing, settling for looser,
wetter beach, indenting prints
that coax up squishes, spray a little.

Splayed toes strike
with the weight of a running man,
forming ridges. The rhythm
of his body earned by years
of daily routine, measured
angles of hips, knees, ankles
powers energy down, forming

tide-line hollows, quick to vanish.
His muscles stretch, tighten over
weathered joints like the shells
of clams or oysters, letting only
carefully chosen nutrients pass.
He drives hard, pushing forward,
striving to overcome the decades.

TIME—THE GAME OF LIFE

Hours are the great gamblers,
      dictate the rules,
      name the game,
      bet against you.

Minutes try to bluff the big guys,
      limit their draw,
      smile slyly,
      it doesn't work.

Seconds are poker chips
      fingered into piles,
      valuable for winners,
      no one wins.

You have only one option:
      give up on everything,
      bet your whole stake,
      leave the game early.

After all, it's your funeral.

VIEW FROM ABOVE

My mother floated
above me, said, *let's fly*
for a while, my child,
and we did. I rode her
slipstream, looked down,

saw my childhood home, repainted an ugly green,
the schools where I learned the pain of being young,
the orthodox synagogue, our wedding all in Hebrew,
promises we never understood,

hospital rooms—a computer
connected to radiation needles,
an octopus of plastic tubes,
an I.V. dripping into a papery hand,

a mausoleum—private,
silent behind closed doors,
my husband's body on a gurney.
My fingers touched his face,
committed death to memory.

My mother moved on,
refused to look down,
or recognize that I was there.
Places rushed by, a paper tablet
flipped to simulate motion.
Flailing, bruised, I landed
without her.

WEE HOURS

2–3–4 a.m. Misnamed, they are huge,
formidable, press down on me, sit on my head.
Big, black bottoms pillow over me, soft,
cover my eyes. Through quivering black,
I sense a pulse, lightless, but I imagine
a spark, a flicker, then it is gone.

I hear small mysterious sighs.
I feel breath knotting like a rag in my throat,
harsh with dryness. Sheets rise with shallow
breaths, arm extended to reach for sleep.
Deep breath in through the nose, count inhales.
Deep exhales through the nose, count exhales.

Smells almost remembered.
Tastes nearly recalled. I remember
his voice from long ago, "You are a delight
becoming." This was to be a new
beginning, then he disappeared, left echoes
floating back from time to time.

Rooms in my head fill, empty; trails wind away,
send familiar bodies, faces to match,
patched into frames on my mind's wall.
I dream I can discover what I lost,
find the missing part of me,
if I could only remember what it was.

WHEN CANDLES ARE NOT ENOUGH

The red ball of fire backlights
strips of black clouds,
apocalyptic knights
foreshadowing deeper thoughts.

The vastness of space,
unfathomed, lies deep
behind the solar furnace.
Riders of the black clouds
drag out of history,
out of the valley of death
the unforgotten, tortured
souls of the six million.

WHEN ONE WORD IS NOT ENOUGH

even the wise can misinterpret
or take another meaning.
One word repeated
shifts its shape, picks up
a strange distorted sound.

A single phrase, limited,
fearful of its demanding job,
can fail to get its message through.

A sentence may need companions
to give it strength in argument;
a paragraph may fill in some holes,
open up others.

A page is just long
enough to offer more
than one idea, and,
more important,
requests and reasons,
or explanations,
threats, and promises.

The wise need only listen
and care enough
to try to understand.

SIX CANDLES

November 9th, 2003. On a cool, comfortable day
in Santa Barbara, a crowd hears a woman
reconstruct Kristallnacht from her memories.

On a wind-chilled November 9th in 1938,
Berlin, a thirteen-year-old walked home
from school, past familiar shops, past her
synagogue, stopped aghast. The building
was ablaze—with fire, not lights—people
ran through the street, women begged, cried,
uniformed men screamed "throw the pigs
into the fire"—what pigs, no animals here,
only people. Jewish people, horrified,
unbelieving, grabbed each other, ran for life.
The girl escaped, dashed back to school,
panicked, ran home. Her family fought
to stay together, kept on running.

Today, she tells us about the years between,
resettling, marriage, successes and pains. She
thanks us for being here, for her life, her children,
grandchildren, for witnessing this memorial.
I read forty stories of that night, see old photos.
All are sheathed in glass, bound with metal,
hinged as forty books, a permanent display,
a reminder of what can never be forgotten.

The ceremony ends. For those who did not
survive, for survivors who are not here,
her grandchildren light six candles.
One for each million.

WHITE HOURS

Tiny noises, crushed under the weight of echoes,
        are amplified by Stanley's inner ear.

                A dead lover, shrouded, seems to stand
                in the frame of Janet's window.

Old grudges leer again, unsettled, disputing
        Stanley's careful compromises.

                Uncommittable crimes tiptoe up the carpeted
                stairs, constricting Janet's breath.

Muscles twitch in memory of old pains. Stanley's
        bruising fall was days ago.

                Janet feels the bump under the skin, the needle's
                burning from yesterday's treatment.

Stanley and Janet conjure up all the old tricks:
        he attempts another crossword,
        she rereads an unremembered novel,
        they both breathe deep yoga nasal breaths,
        replay memories in reverse almost to the birth canal.

The night bangs its head against the white hours
        until it is exhausted.

Stanley and Janet surrender to the light,
        stretch out their arms,
        roll away from each other.

THE CONCERT

This music, revered by time, its
structure honored, unchanging,
revitalized by emphasis, dilution,
timing, blows through me fresh
and clean and adds a tang to the
blandness of the day.

My personal specters are raised
to eye level so I can ponder
familiarity at leisure, feel the
losses retreat one more time to
a safe, moderate distance, just this
side of the closet that secretes them.

My body sways unbidden to the
tempo of the current force. There
is enough strength here to wash
away ordinary dreads and duties.

I command the musicians to play
forever. They ignore me, continue
on to conclude, to be on their way.

When the music stops, coldness
follows, and the structure of
pretense implodes in my brain.

As I walk away, I realize I have
already forgotten the melodies.

WHITE SILENCE

Metal curtain rods
split the ceiling's
diffuse light
into oblique lines
across his cheeks.

His unblinking eyes
fixed on the television.
Every actor was his son,
every story his own.
His mind's margin
remembered aunts,
uncles as being alive—
none were.
Some days
he understood
they wouldn't come.

Late one night,
as the hours turned
white, a machine signaled
body failure, dinged
a small sound through
hospital corridors.
Patients, silent,
held their breath.

On the next shift,
the charge nurse
saw the empty bed,
could not recall
the face.

BLUE

There will be no
millennia
to turn atoms into
ooze, ooze into cells.
A trickster is needed
to stretch nuclei
into twisted strands,
the helixes of life,
all the way to homo
sapiens of every
persuasion.

Blue morpho,
an airborne survivor,
its butterfly wings
dressed in metallic
blue luster,
will spread them wide,
lift its body up, over
to drained land
where fecundity
is essential
and begins the process.

As bloodlines develop,
entwine, father, mother
spin off tribal feather
bearers. Some people
will despise the feathers

of alien tribes, burn them.
Some will vow to destroy
believers in a godhead
borne on two crossed

wooden stakes, or in a god
called Yahweh, or those
who choose a different path
to honor the prophet who leapt
skyward from the black rock.

Some will enforce
decapitation
of nonbelievers,
celebrate their deaths,
insist, in the name
of the honored
Manufacturer, that
all mothers of all men
will be closeted,
loosed
only when wrapped
in blue, head to foot.

They will suck air
through screens
cupped like
an insect's mouth,
progenitors
of daughters born
to wear the same
draperies that drip
from rain on the outside,
from sweat on the inside.

Blue morpho,
reconsider
phylogeny.

LISTEN

I trick myself. Believe
I create my own harmony,
dissonances, inventiveness,
a display of unexpected virtuosity,
variety of phrasing,
until all codas are exhausted
when I confront my orchestrated life.

I bridge from violin to violin,
titillated by trills,
smiling as trombones chuckle
at apologetic French horns.
Oboes with human inflections
simper at the clarinets,
the sorrowful bassoons;
the heavy-handed timpani
flatten them all.

Final chords; I listen, anticipate
the end, still caught by surprise.
Nothing for it but to leave the hall
to ghosts of musicians, audiences,
gather my things, my stuff,
my brain hangs back,
replays melodies,
the memory of pleasure.

VIII
Rarely Blue
Poems from the 90s

VENICE CANALS

No Doge palaces here—a Hollywood
developer's choice reclaimed
from failure by trend-fraught Californians.

Some of these Venetians drive sleek
power boats (rowing is for gyms),
gliding over bits of broken wooden
mini-docks, pickerel weeds, mucky debris.

Ducks—visible residents—paddle,
hunt worms, smear sidewalks with
slimy droppings. Protected, the ducks
are not for eating, but for fun to feed,
enriching slow water. This ambiance
not inclusive of unshaven men or dirt-
encrusted women propped up
next to an empty bottle.

Bridges, high-arched, are slatted,
designed for cell-phone photos, not
for lingering. Houses, stuccoed
in pastels, have balconies, fenced
yards, alarm systems.

Nowhere on the canals can homeless
find shelter, so some still huddle
for the night, cocooned in sleeping
bags on beach sands, hoping to
escape detection by police 'copters
or early morning dogs.

Vagrants and dogs are not welcome here.

'ROUND MIDNIGHT

He covered the distance from Detroit to Chicago in record time,
      ready to hit the jazz clubs, hit nothing else.
He dropped school, enlisted in the army, made himself
      a moving target, big but too fast to hit.
He took a chance, married a girl as screwed up as he was,
      managed to make it work most of the time.

A careless driver, he was king of the road with his kids
      cowering in the back seat.
      Drank a little,
      smoked a lot,
      wrapped himself in a corporate blanket,
      convinced of his immortality.

He was surprised, 'round midnight, when with a whimper
half of his mind slipped away, leaving half his body
paralyzed in bed with a tangle of blankets
and a puzzled look.

HEAVEN

Take only small bills.
God will not make change.
Exchange rates are regulated.
Everyone pays a commission.
Most borrow from St. Peter
to pay St. Paul and take advantage
of a lower percent of interest.
All the lovers you had when you were
young will live only inside your
head, just as they do now.
The little ones, and sometimes
the elderly ones, dirty their diapers.
Someone has to clean them up.
Dry skin, acne, and dandruff persist.
There are different races, languages,
religions. People who hated those
who are different still do.
Copulation occurs at any time, in any place,
but old men still prefer young women.
Grass needs cutting.
Trees need trimming.
Vermin need extermination, but resist.
The sky is sometimes gray, sometimes
brown, but rarely blue.
Some people never win, and they
have kinfolk who always lose.
If it was broken when it arrived,
no one here can fix it.
This will continue forever;
everyone is too scared to
do anything about it.
God might sue.

There is no other place.
This is all there is.
The bottom line:

No matter how great the yearning
or how intense the disillusion,
no one is allowed to leave.
They got what they prayed for.

MIRRORS

Bodies in our mirrors, waxy-smooth
with unlined surfaces, gentle curves,
well-proportioned, not quite Barbie yet,
but asymptotic to that ageless goddess,
we reflect on thee.

We raise the banner:
WELCOME, SLENDER YOUTH
(the cherished image well within the realm
of the achievable, since medicine has
searched, researched, experimented,
braved insurance companies and lawsuits
to present us with our new
elective visages and shapes).

Wise women said of physical appearance, "Beauty is:
              as beauty does,
              is in the eye of the beholder,
              is thin, skin deep."
Then, they embraced the Beast to change
him, not to take him as he was. His
physiognomy caused them uneasiness.
The princess would not wed an unkissed frog,
even though he was the Tadpole King.
Cinderella had to dress in satin, lace, and glass
to satisfy the prince's notion of success.

Gray hairs once earned respect. The brow,
furrowed by thought, was crowned with laurel.
Eyes and lips that folded into wrinkles
when they smiled made people smile back.
When the finger of an acquaintance slowly peeled
layers off, a jewel (or an onion) was revealed.

Now, television channels different standards.
Magazines flaunt advertisers' images.

423

Some rush to alter everything at once,
believing the persona is their definition.

Do not go gently to be liposucked.
Rage against the drawing of the knife.
The mirror has no way to understand
what it is that makes us fairest in the land.

THE CRUISE

Hypnotic, white-frothed, propeller-churned waves
draw like a magnet, like moths to a flame,
the poets, the dreamers, the unloved, the flounderers,
the loners whose encapsulated lives force them
into isolation, then into the ship's wake.

Icy gasps   a magnified scope closing through
a blackened green tunnel,
implosion lit by a rocket's glare—
            a roar of silence

Looking upward through refracted light, seeing the
faces peering over the rail, they seem warped, misshapen;
the hands reaching downward, the futile throw of
lifelines helpful only to those who stayed behind.
So far above the water, there was really nothing to
be done, but they felt better for having tried, self-satisfied
at making any gesture to assist a drowning man.

Arms clutch solid, dry flesh, wrap each other in a shield,
teeth chatter, clattering like needles knitting a pattern
of the life of a stranger. They push across the bleak deck
wondering at a precious promise, at an insubstantial
something they seem to have misplaced.
Jostling, they move inside toward the pink upholstery,
polished chrome, deep-piled carpets, waxed or marble floors,
toward the reality of silk or plastic plants, the repetitive
tape of a golden oldie, piped into every space, the stiff,
black and white penguin suits of the waiters.

At the first seating, one place is vacant,
one setting unused. No one who sits
at that table can say the name,
remember the face, or recall the voice
of the person who is no longer there.
The captain's voice interrupts the chatter.

He requests a moment of silence for one
who is missing, for one of the poets, the dreamers,
the unloved, the flounderers, the loners.

TO A FRIEND ON THE DEATH OF HER INFANT SON

His cries and his silences were
the notes of a song for you,
especially,
to hear and understand.
The song was what he was meant
to bring you. A song to deepen
understanding of yourself
and of the world,
of the landscape inside,
the landscape outside.

His was the music of growth,
of change, of selfish need
and selfless giving.
Now, his song is part of you.
It will live inside of you.
It belongs to you.
You have the choice to share it
with your family, your friends,
and anyone else who comes
your way.

It is a lovely song.
You have received a gift.
Use it well, wisely,
and in peace.

THE SHIP CLOCK

The clock face was centered in a
wooden hull flattened to conform
to the top of the spinet. The sails
were of flimsy metal with reef
points of tin wire attached to
silver masts. The wires twanged
in sympathy with the chords I
banged out on the piano.

Czerny etudes were taught to me
by a balding man with a pencil-
thin moustache who smelled of
strong soap. His soft hands were
casual on the stool but they
managed to touch my body.
Confused, I shifted away but
his hands followed. Unable to
explain, I refused to keep going.

I had to study music on my own.
The ship clock monitored my
progress, which slowed, and my
ambition, which disappeared.

The ropes of the clock resonated
on, but it could only watch.

I played only for myself, even
my parents stopped listening.

Music is still a consolation,
but the ship clock vanished
many years ago.

REBORN POETS SOCIETY

Today is the day the poets read
again after a long silence. They
were poets of commitment, of
conscience. When the drums were
stilled, they amputated their
tongues, sewed their eyelids shut.
This radical surgery excised them
from the corps of moderns, the
body of coffeehouse readers.

Too short a time for history,
time enough for nostalgia,
time to resurrect their craft,
they found themselves
objects of curiosity,
owners of names
remembered slightly, if at all.

The audience listened, laughing
at the funny parts, silent when
slight bitterness appeared,
reading the program again,
looking out the window at the greenery outside.

Lest reacquaintance be forgot,
or never brought to mind,
they gathered in the garden
to share a glass of wine.

Old friends reminisced, hugged,
kissed, told factoids no one else
remembered. Young ones listened,
curious, polite, put down their
glasses, said goodbye, and left
as though it were an ordinary
Sunday afternoon.

ABOUT THE AUTHOR

Joyce and Art Stein, early 1950s

My mother, Joyce Stein, was born Elaine Joyce Marcus on February 10, 1931, in Los Angeles, California. Four days after her birth, her name was officially changed to Joyce Elaine. Her father, Edward, was a first-generation immigrant from Kiev who came over as a baby; her mother, Victoria, was born in Chicago, the youngest of ten in a family newly arrived in the US from Liverpool. Joyce was the eldest of two girls, with Carole coming along in 1934. Edward sold display cases and refrigeration units to markets and managed to stay employed throughout the depression. Victoria (known by her grandchildren as Grandma Vic) was helped by her mother, Grandma Eva, who lived with the Marcus family in Hollywood until she passed away when Joyce was twelve.

Joyce was smart. She went to Fairfax High in Hollywood and started at UCLA at age sixteen. She met my father, Arthur Stein, at UCLA, and they were married in 1952; she was twenty-one, and he was

Stein family, early 1960s

431

Stein family, early 1960s

twenty-four. They were into left-wing politics and jazz and waited a bit to have kids, but then had three in quick succession: Abbott in 1958, Adam in 1960, and me, Barney, in 1962. While Art pursued a career in hospital administration, Joyce worked in offices before the kids were born and went back to work in the late sixties for the LA Unified School District, working in HR for several years before becoming a high school math teacher in the mid-seventies until her retirement in the early 1990s. Art had a major stroke in 1988 but lived for thirteen more years, at first in rehab, later in a VA nursing home; Joyce pursued her dream of travel on her own, often with groups, but never with my father. Still, she visited him regularly when she was in town.

Joyce with lemur, Madagascar, 2000

My mother was a firebrand. She worked in local politics, consumed every kind of art, traveled to the third world many times, to the Gobi Desert, to the Okavango Delta, to the Iranian mud city of Bam before it was destroyed, to the Three Rivers Gorge in China before it was flooded. She camped out in the Australian Outback when she was over seventy-five years old. She was endlessly social and loved meeting new people, managing to communicate with hand signals if no common language, however broken, could be found. She could worry with the best of

Joyce in the Gobi Desert, Mongolia, 2006

them, but she really wasn't timid. At all. I'm not sure what led her to poetry. She wasn't inclined to it when we were growing up, and she was always the math person: practical, technical, able to grapple with

Joyce in Iran, 2000

any complex restaurant bill. She even, apparently, played Dungeons and Dragons with some of her students. But then, she was passionate about what she believed in. She was a keen observer of life, and she saw a lot of it. Joyce took to writing with gusto in the mid-nineties, producing hundreds of poems over the next twenty years. This collection contains as many of them as I could find. I did not think this great work of hers should be lost. She left us in 2017, a few weeks shy of her eighty-sixth birthday. She is missed and remembered often.

www.ingramcontent.com/pod-product-compliance
Lightning Source LLC
Chambersburg PA
CBHW030310100426
42812CB00002B/644